Let's Talk and Play

Eileen DiStasio-Clark

Contents

Dedication

With Great Love and Appreciation to
Those Who Have and Do Bless My Life.

My Family:
Joseph DeStasio Sr. & Miriam Lucille Baragone DeStasio
My Late Parents

Andrea Jean DeStasio McIntosh
My Older Sister and Their Families

Joseph DeStasio Jr.
My Younger and Only Brother and Their Families

Donna Marie DeStasio Wagner
My Younger Sister and   Their Families

My Children:
Eileen, Rebekah, Rachel,
S. Michael, Jennifer, Sharon, Tara,
Stephanie, Apryll, Mikaelah, & M. Trevor
and
THEIR Families!!

i

Acknowledgments

First and foremost, I express, deeply, my sincere gratitude to our Heavenly Father for blessing me with the gift and talent of writing! I know I could not do what I do without His assistance.

I also want to acknowledge and express gratitude to the members of my birth family—Joseph Sr., Miriam, Andrea, Joseph Junior, and Donna. All the experiences of my childhood years, experiences that taught me so very much and enabled me to reveal my true self to myself, came about through my experiences and relationships with them.

And, of course, it goes without saying, but I will say it anyway: I also want to acknowledge and note my gratitude to my children, Eileen, Rebekah, Rachel, S. Michael, Jennifer, Sharon, Tara, Stephanie, Apryll, Mikaelah, and M. Trevor, and their families! Through multiple things they said to me, over multiple years, I finally came to the realization that Heavenly Father gave me the gift of writing and opened the doors to these experiences because He knew that by sharing them with others, others could feel His love, too. And He definitely wants us all to know that He, Heavenly Father, Heavenly Mother, and Jehovah truly do love us!!!

About the Author

Eileen DiStasio-Clark was born on September 6, 1953, in West Reading, Pennsylvania to Joseph and Miriam DeStasio. She is the second oldest of four children; her siblings being Andrea McIntosh, Joseph DeStasio Junior, and Donna Wagner. Eileen now lives in Missouri, and is the mother of 11 children— 9 girls and 2 boys: Eileen, Rebekah, Rachel, S. Michael, Jennifer, Sharon, Tara, Stephanie, Apryll, Mikaelah, and M. Trevor.. As a member of The Church of Jesus Christ of Latter-Day Saints, she has served in various positions, teaching, leading, and ministering to children, youth, and adults. Eileen established, and is the President/Director of Pursuit of Excellence Institute of Family Education, a non-profit organization focused on the family. Presently, she holds an AA, a BA, and an MA in Clinical Psychology and is working on the completion of her Doctoral degree.

Let's Talk and Play

Talks Prepared for and Delivered in
Sunday School, Sacrament, and Special Meetings

A Play Prepared for and Presented in a
Special Youth Program

A Puppet Show Prepared for and Presented in a
Cub Scout Meeting

A Play Adapted from a
Sacrament Presentation

A Play Prepared and Presented in the
Women's Organization ~Relief Society

By

Eileen DiStasio-Clark
And
Aubrey Johnson
And
S. Michael Clark Junior

1

Introduction

In The Church of Jesus Christ of Latter-Day Saints, the first Sunday of each month is Fast Sunday. Those who can, are encouraged to fast for the purpose of coming closer to our Heavenly Parents and our Savior, Jesus Christ, and to be able to be endowed with the blessings that we need, and blessings for others.

On that Sunday, our Sacrament Meeting is known as Fast and Testimony Meeting, and any member who so desires to do so, is welcomed to share with the congregation their testimony of the truthfulness of the gospel and the church, and experiences they have had that exemplify the blessings they have received though and because of the living of these truths. On the other Sundays, as evidence of the marvelous blessings that are available to us, members, by invitation, are given the opportunity to share true Principles of the Gospel of Jesus Christ, and evidence of these truths through their experiences of living them, with each other through the deliverance of talks in our Sacrament Meetings.

Through the divine inspiration that comes to our leaders in response to prayerful considerations, two or three members of the Ward or Branch are invited to present talks on a given gospel topic. Those invited to speak in these meetings, study the topic assigned for their talk, and pray for guidance from our Heavenly Father, so as to know what is best and most needed to be shared. Herein, are a few talks, definitely not all of them, that I delivered in Sacrament Meetings in several different Wards, which I attended.

ALSO

I think I was born with an interest in 'pretending.' As a very young child, I, with my siblings and cousins, whenever anyone suggested it, created 'make-believe' stories, and shared them with everyone any time we had the opportunity to do so arose. Now, I probably do not need to say this, but I will anyway, I was usually the "suggester."

When I was in Elementary School, our teachers often had us perform, on a voluntary basis, skits in some of our classes. Of course, I always volunteered!

In High School, both Junior and Senior, we had drama plays every year, and I was in every one of them. Sometimes, I tried out for a part. Sometimes, I was asked to play a part. But in every play, I had a part.

Well, that love of performance was also accompanied by a love for creating. As soon as I could read and write, beginning in first grade, I began writing stories, poems, songs, and plays. Most of them I wrote by myself. A few of them I wrote with someone else. Almost always, that someone else was a family member. Now, many of those plays got lost over time, but a few remained and still do. And those are the plays that are contained herein.

It is my sincere joy to share them with you and my true hope that you will enjoy, utilize, and share them with others. But remember to share them and utilize them in the way they were written—no amendments, alterations, or adaptations of any kind!

Note: The songs mentioned in two of the plays: "A Poor Wayfaring Man of Grief" and

"Once Upon a Might Have Begun"—"A Poor Wayfaring Man of Grief",

"As Sisters in Zion", and "Abide With Me"—can be found on the website of The Church of Jesus Christ of Latter-Day Saints.

Magnifying Your Callings

By Eileen DiStasio-Clark

1981

Reading Ward in Reading, Berks, Pennsylvania

"Glory Be", 'The Apostles' Creed", "Hail Mary", "O Jesus" . . . These are but a few of the over 50 prayers I was taught, and used, as a Catholic. Every morning, I attended 6:00 Mass, and then recited the 43 prayers of the Stations of the Cross. Every night, I recited the 120 prayers of the Rosary. With few exceptions, I recited about 168 prayers daily. Yet, for all the recitations, the Heavens seemed closed to me.

As a Latter-Day Saint, I was taught to converse, that is, to pray conversationally, with Heavenly Father, and I have been blessed to hear, see, feel, and understand the answers to my prayers.

Throughout my life, my greatest loves and focuses have always been God and Family. As a Catholic, I had to choose between them. To serve God, and the church, as a nun, I could not marry or have children. To have a family, I could not serve God or the church fully.

As a Latter-Day Saint, not only have I been able to do both, but to serve my Heavenly Father most fully, and for my eternal benefit, I need both!

5

There are so very many gifts and blessings we receive from the gospel! Perhaps, more often than not, the Father blesses us beyond our worthiness. Do we really earn ALL that we receive? Or, through His mercy and love, does the Father bless us with gifts? So much is given to us, yet, so little is asked of us. And that which is asked—obedience and service—again benefits us.

Not enough could be said about the importance of obedience. It is not a difficult concept. The Father, in the Scriptures, states, "Do it!" The Father, through the Prophets, said, "Live it and do not customize it!" The Father knew what He was saying when He spoke, and who of us is qualified to amend any of that?

Now, about service ~

The much-quoted scripture from . . .

Mosiah 2:17

And behold, I tell you these things that ye may learn **wisdom**; that ye may learn that when ye are in the **service** of your **fellow** beings, ye are only in the service of your God.

. . . clearly, and simply explains how we serve Heavenly Father: we serve each other!

Serve . . . what does that mean?

Webster says . . .

6

To assist: To be of use: To hold an office: To wait on people:

To do something for another . . .

For another? Hmmm, obeying the commandments is NOT service! Crucial as that is—and it definitely is!—obedience, alone, is not enough.

Obedience is what we do for ourselves. Service is what we do for others. Since none of us is fully capable of overcoming ourselves, our trials, our setbacks and challenges, our handicaps, or of obtaining exaltation totally on our own, we need each other!! Service, then, becomes as crucial as uncompromised obedience!!

Temporal vocations and accomplishments have value only in as much as they relate to our eternal progression and assist us in fulfilling or achieving divine responsibilities and goals. But service in the home and at church is spiritually significant and therefore is the **most** valuable service which can be rendered!

How devoted are you to your family? How devoted are you to your church callings? What positions do you hold—secretary, parent, sibling, counselor, bishop, teacher, husband, chorister, president, wife, leader..? Who called you to these positions?

Do you think you chose them yourself? Do you think you were given your calling because no one else wanted it? Maybe you consider friendship to be the basis of your election.

Well, Brothers, I suppose you did ask your wife to marry you. Sisters, apparently, you chose to accept the proposal. But I believe Heavenly Father is far more involved in our personal lives than we readily realize. And the children? It is my testimony that spiritual selection is more a part of our family composition than is biology.

Indeed, the Bishop, or one of his counselors spoke to you about your church calling, but ALL calls come from God!

Alma 13: 3 & 4 teaches . . .

3. And this is the manner after which they were ordained—

being called and prepared from the foundation of the world according to the foreknowledge of God, on account of their exceeding faith and good works; in the first place being left to choose good or evil; therefore, they have chosen good, and exercising exceedingly great faith, are called with a holy calling, yea, with that holy calling which was prepared with, and according to, a preparatory redemption for such.

4. And thus they have been called to this holy calling on account of their faith, while others would reject the Spirit of God on account of the hardness of their hearts and blindness of

their minds, while, if it had not been for this they might have had as great privilege as their brethren.

Maybe others were offered the calling before you were. Heavenly Father knew what their response would be. He does not employ the trial-and-error method. Perhaps what was offered to them was meant to serve some other good purpose in their lives. You are where the Father, not anyone else, called you to be, and you are the person He wanted in that calling at this time. He knows what you can offer, and what you can gain, if you serve well!

Magnify your calling! Let us go back to **Webster,** where we learn that to magnify is... **To make something greater: To increase in significance . . .**

How do you make a calling greater? How does a calling make you greater?

A teacher can just show up for class, play a game, read out of a manual . . . Or a teacher can be well prepared with a good interactive, multisensory lesson, attend in-service and council meetings, form a personal relationship with students, etc.

A secretary can just fill out reports and send them to the Stake . . . Or a secretary can share ideas with the president, create extras, which will acknowledge the members being served, go the extra mile to help those with whom he or she serves, attend in-service, council, and presidency meetings, and more...

A librarian can just hang around the library, handing out crayons, chalk, and scissors . . . Or a librarian can seek ways to assist others with advanced preparation, set up resource displays, and teach others how to implement the resources of the library . . .

No matter the calling, there is a way to simply do the minimum that must be done, making our callings as small as they can be, or do all that is required for spiritual performance, seeking ways, through love, commitment, and creativity, to go the extra miles, magnifying them, making them as large and involved as stewardship will allow.

Of course, it is difficult to magnify a calling if you do not even know what all those responsibilities are. So, when you are called to your position, if the bishop or counselor does not define the calling for you, ask him to do so. If those you are serving under do not come to you for further orientation, go to them. And, always, and of course, go to the Father.

Then, as you serve, make sure you attend all meetings associated with your calling: in-service meetings, council meetings, presidency meetings, leadership meetings, etc., and counsel with your leaders and with those you are serving.

Sometimes, you may feel inadequate for your calling. That is not possible. No special education or training is required to serve the Lord.

Doctrine and Covenants 4: 3 says . . .

Therefore, if ye have desires to serve God, ye are <u>called</u> to the work

Desire to serve is the qualifier in the Lord's Kingdom. The Lord then does His own training.

I Corinthians 1: 26 & 27 says . . .

26. For ye see your calling, brethren, how that not many wise men after   the flesh, not many mighty, not many noble, *are called:*

27. But God hath chosen the foolish things of the world to confound the   wise, and God hath chosen the weak things of the world to confound the things which are mighty;

The world's training is not necessarily necessary for service, and may not be helpful in the Lord's Kingdom. That is why we have meetings, so the Lord can train us in His ways. We cannot get that eternally valuable training, if we do not attend our meetings.

Without that training, it is more difficult to serve well, and impossible to magnify or be magnified by your calling. When you serve well, and receive the Lord's training, you are blessed

11

and become a better, greater person, and are able to serve in a better, greater way.

Doctrine and Covenants 9: 14 promises . . .

Stand fast in the work wherewith I have called you, and a hair of your head shall not be lost, and you shall be <u>lifted up</u> at the last day. Amen.

and

Doctrine and Covenants 105: 35 says . . .

There has been a day of calling, but the time has come for a day of choosing; and let those be chosen that are worthy.

Contrarily, for those who do not serve well . . .

Doctrine and Covenants 95: 5 & 6 reminds us . . .

5. But behold, verily I say unto you, that there are many who have been ordained among you, whom I have called, but few of them are <u>chosen</u>.

6. They who are not chosen have sinned a very grievous sin, in that they are <u>walking</u> in <u>darkness</u> at noon-day.

Perhaps you think you are too busy for all these responsibilities and meetings . . .

John 15: 16 reminds us . . .

Ye have not chosen me, but I have chosen you, and ordained you, that ye should go and bring forth fruit, and that your fruit should remain:

That whatsoever ye shall ask of the Father in my name, he may give it to you.

Since it was the Father who called you, when you are too busy for your calling, are you too busy for the Lord? He knows your circumstances, challenges, commitments, and abilities before He calls you. He calls you anyway. He knows there is a way for you to fulfill that call. If you do not know what that way is, ask Him!

When we accept a call, we promise to serve. That is the purpose of callings—to serve—to do the work of the Father!

Isaiah 6:8 reminds us of another promise made to us . . .

Also, I heard the voice of the Lord, saying, Whom shall I <u>send</u>, and who will go for us? Then said I, here *am* I; <u>send</u> me.

Evaluate yourself for a moment. If the Lord answered His call to be our redeemer in the same manner you serve in your calling—whatever it is—where would we be now?!

Perhaps you think your calling is not that important; it's just church.

THINK AGAIN!!!!!!

Matthew 18: 6 identifies how important church service is . . .

But whoso shall offend one of these little ones which believe in me, it were better for him that a millstone was hanged about his neck, and that he were drowned in the depth of the sea.

Little one? Who are they? Children?

Bruce R. McConkie describes little ones this way . . .

". . . children are our Father's children. He has entrusted them to us for a time and a season. Our appointment is to bring them up in light and truth so they will qualify to return to his Eternal Presence."

Now, let us not forget that all of us are children, not just of our earthly parents, but of our Heavenly Parents, too. Ergo, we are all those children.

So, it seems our callings, whatever they may be, are meant to be taken most seriously! And the utmost care is to be given to the execution of those callings! The world, life, and Satan, have great power to draw you away from your responsibilities to each other and your promise to the Father. But when you are set apart for your calling, you are given a shield against those influences.

President Spencer W. Kimball said . . .

"The more we serve our fellowmen in appropriate ways, the more substance there is to our souls. We become more significant individuals as we serve others. We become more

substantive as we serve others—indeed, it is easier to "find" ourselves because there is so much more of us to find!"

So, you are called by God to your positions. You are offered all the training and blessings you need to fulfill those callings. You are shielded from the influences of the world as you serve faithfully. There are no reasons we cannot keep the promises and commitments we made to the Father when we accepted our calls.

We are or will be endowed with everything we need to magnify those callings and thereby be magnified by them. Now, we simply must decide and commit to doing it; remember always . . .

Matthew 25: 40 tells us . . .

And the King shall answer and say unto them, Verily I say unto you, Inasmuch as ye have done it unto one of the least of these my brethren, ye have done it unto me.

In the name of Jesus Christ, Amen!

Perfection – Fact or Fiction

By Eileen DiStasio-Clark

Around 1986

Jacksonville Sixth Ward in Jacksonville, Duval, Florida

There are 93 scriptural references under the Topical Guide heading, "Perfection, Perfect, Perfectly", and additional heading references. It would appear that the Lord had a lot to say to us about being perfect!

Is it truly possible to be perfect? What is meant by this statement, in

Deuteronomy 18:13: "Thou shalt be perfect with the Lord thy God."

Or

3 Nephi 12: 48: "Therefore, I would that ye should be perfect, even as I, or your

Father, who is in Heaven is perfect."

Or

Colossians 4:12: ". . . stand perfect and complete in the will of God."

Or

Genesis 17:1: "I am the Almighty God; walk before Me and be thou perfect."

Or

Matthew 5: 48: "Be ye therefore perfect, even as your Father, which is in

Heaven is perfect."

Or

I Kings 8:61: "Let your heart, therefore, be perfect with the Lord our God, to

walk in His statutes, and to keep His commandments."

And

Job 1:1: "…Job …was perfect and upright, and one that feared God and eschewed evil."

There is a good indication that the Lord does want us to be perfect! But can we be?

Well, what does it mean to be perfect?

In the **World Book Dictionary**, perfect and perfection carry these definitions:

Perfect:

having no faults; not spoiled at any point; without defect;

completely skilled; expert; thoroughly learned or acquired;

having all its parts there; whole; complete; exact; precise; entire; utter; total; pure; unmixed; unalloyed.

Perfection:

Faultless quality; highest excellence; a quality, trait, or accomplishment of a high degree of excellence; the highest or most perfect degree of a quality or trait.

Job was described as perfect. He was **upright**. According to the second definition in the **World Book Dictionary**, **upright** means **morally good, honest, and righteous.** He feared the Lord. The fourth definition in the **World Book Dictionary** for **fear** is **awe; reverence.** Job **eschewed** evil. **Eschew**, according to the **World Book Dictionary**, means **to keep away from, avoid or shun.**

When we apply the scriptures to these definitions, the resulting definitions of perfection and perfect are:

Perfection:

A complete understanding of, and total commitment to, Heavenly Father's Gospel; living the gospel in its purity, not mixing the gospel with the ideologies of any other religion or with the philosophies or persuasions of man

Perfect:

To Have a complete understanding of, and total commitment to, Heavenly Father's Gospel, living the

18

gospel in its purity, not mixing the gospel with the ideologies of any other religion or with the philosophies or persuasions of man.

When we consider this applied definition, how do we answer the question, 'Is it possible to become perfect?'

Naturally, using any definition, the answer has to be 'Yes!' There are two evidences for this.

First: We know that we can become as Heavenly Father and Heavenly Mother.

They are perfect; therefore, we can become perfect.

Second: If it were not possible for us to become perfect, Heavenly Father would not have commanded us to do so.

However, we must understand that this does not happen with desire alone, or just one prayer, or overnight, or all at once. There is a growth process involved in perfection, and that process may take more time than any of us have in mortality.

Consider this from **Doctrine of Salvation,** compiled by **Bruce R. McConkie:**

"Salvation does not come all at once; we are commanded to be perfect even as our Father in Heaven is perfect. It will take us ages to accomplish this end, for there will be greater progress beyond

the grave, and it will be there that the faithful will overcome all things and receive all things, even the fulness of the Father's glory.

"I believe the Lord meant just what He said; that we should be perfect, as our Father in Heaven is perfect. That will not come all at once, but line upon line, and precept upon precept, example upon example, and even then, not as long as we live in this mortal life, for we will have to go even beyond that grave before we reach that perfection and shall be like God.

"But here we lay the foundation. Here is where we are taught the simple truths of the gospel of Jesus Christ, in this probationary state, to prepare us for that perfection. It is our duty to be better today than we were yesterday, and better tomorrow than we are today. Why? Because

we are on that road, if we are keeping the commandments of the Lord, we are on the road to perfection, and that can only come through obedience and the desire in our hearts to overcome the world."

We begin the growth process here; our attitude and effort, NOW, are of vital significance! If we do not develop the proper attitude or apply continual daily effort to be our best and then some, we will not be able to attain perfection in any life. We cannot compromise the way we live the gospel now, thinking we will be able to live it better in the next life and still attain perfection. It will be too late to begin then.

Though we must begin now, to do our best, daily, living to the full extent of our knowledge and ability, we will not become perfect all at once. Consider this:

A student of the piano is not as accomplished at Level Two as he or she is at Level Five. Yet, at each level—five, two, one, any level—all the songs in the book for that level can be played with perfect rhythm, timing, notation, expression, etc.

In horsemanship, a first-year rider would not be able to perform with the precision of a fourth- or sixth-year rider. However, as each new skill, balance, posture, hand & wrist position and control, leg & knee position and pressure, seat, etc., are learned, they can be mastered.

The third-grade mathematics student will not be able to solve an engineering or astronomy equation. Yet, again, each new concept—addition, subtraction, multiplication, division, fractions, etc.—can be learned with complete comprehension and functional skills.

In each of these, and in all endeavors, progression is toward a greater goal. Each level of progression, each stage of the growth process, can be completed to its own perfection, a perfection that leads to the ability to use skill and knowledge to live and perform with greater ease and more enjoyment. This development to perfection on one level makes the next level attainable.

I have identified seven stages of progression or growth in the perfection process, which I call **ICY YAAMAS**. It goes like this:

I = INFANT – just introduced to a gospel principle or practice

C = CHILD – limited, but growing understanding of gospel principles and practices

Y = YOUTH – understanding of gospel principles and practices but commitment may be absent, not yet developed

Y = YOUNG A = ADULT – strong understanding of gospel principles and practices with weak, but strengthening commitment that is developing and growing

A = ADULT – complete or perfect understanding of gospel principles and practices with growing commitment and selective living

M = MATURE A = ADULT – perfect understanding of gospel principles and practices with strong commitment and lifestyle changes in the process of being made

S = SAGE – perfect understanding of gospel principles and practices; compelling commitment; changes of lifestyle and character

These stages of growth are not determined by age or tenure of church membership. With each principle or practice, everyone begins as an infant. We can be an infant with one principle and a mature adult with another. In fact, at any given moment in our lives, we are probably all **ICY YAAMAS**, i.e., a combination of all the stages, each in connection with a different principle or practice.

Maybe you were just introduced to the principle of Zion living or the United Order. You know nothing about it. It is not a part of your knowledge. Here you are, an **Infant.**

You know a bit more, however, about Eternal marriage. You are not planning to attend the temple because you do not know of its importance yet. You just heard about Eternal marriage. It sounds good, but it is just a concept. You are a **Child.**

Yet, at the same time, you are a **Youth** with full understanding of the Law of the Sabbath. You know you should not shop, eat in a restaurant, or go to the football game on Sunday. You also know you should be attending church, all of it, every Sunday, but you do not have a full commitment to do so.

You understand very well, the Word of Wisdom. You want to live it, but it is hard, and you cannot achieve it completely. You are a **Young Adult**.

Now, you understand fully, the reason we are instructed to indulge only in wholesome entertainment. You desire very much to follow this directive and sometimes you do, but only when it is easy. If the content of that R or PG-13 movie appeals to you, you will go see it. You are just an **Adult** with this practice.

As a **Mature Adult**, with the principle of service, you fully comprehend the need and responsibility to faithfully fulfill your calling, no matter what it is. You very greatly desire to magnify your calling and go the extra mile. You almost always make the necessary changes in your life or schedule in order to fulfill that commitment.

With tithing, you are a **Sage**! There is no challenge to pay for it. You pay tithing because you love and trust the Lord and it would never occur to you to not pay your tithing, even in the most dire financial circumstances.

Ergo, you are and **ICY YAAMAS**, and you are on your way to perfection!

Perfection is a fact! It involves a growth process which takes a very long, long time. Perfection in all doctrines, policies, principles, and practices of the gospel does not occur simultaneously. We can be perfect in some things while still progressing in others.

The basis or foundation for perfection is a complete understanding of and total commitment to Heavenly Father, coupled with the action of living, to our utmost ability, harmoniously with His will.

In the name of Jesus Christ, Amen!

Is Perfection Possible

By Eileen DiStasio-Clark

Between 1989 and 1991

Greenville 3rd Ward in Greenville, South Carolina

Or

Gaffney Ward in Gaffney, South Carolina

I wonder if, perhaps, the most detrimental idea in circulation throughout the world is the notion that suggests that we cannot be perfect in this life.

In **Matthew 5: 48**, the Savior directs us to "**<u>Be</u> ye therefore <u>perfect</u>, even as your <u>Father</u> which is in Heaven is <u>perfect</u>.**"

Why would the Lord give us a command that was not possible to be accomplished? Perhaps the confusion is not with our abilities but with the interpretation of the Lord's direction. We are told to be perfect, as Heavenly Father is perfect. How is He perfect? What is perfection? If we understand the answers to these questions, we may then understand that it is possible to be perfect in this life—even now!

Perfectionism is this:

—the doctrine that the perfection of moral character constitutes a person's highest good

—the theological doctrine that a state of freedom from sin
  is

attainable on earth

—a disposition to regard anything short of perfection as
  unacceptable

Perfection is this:

—a freedom from fault or defeat

—the quality or state of being saintly

—an exemplification of supreme excellence

—an unsurpassable degree of accuracy and excellence

Now, we will condense this: perfection is to be perfect. It is to possess a moral character constituted of the person's highest good, achieved in this life, by living free from sin.

Is this possible?

Of course!

As we do our best—our BEST—to live by the commandments, doctrines, precepts, standards, principles, and counsels of the gospel without compromising them, but as they have been given to us, we live a perfect life. Now that does not mean without some mistakes and certainly not without misfortunes, but, nonetheless, still a life of perfection.

Now, you may wonder, 'If I am making mistakes, how can I be like Heavenly Father?'

President Lorenzo Snow, in relating a revelation he had just prior to his mission to England while discussing the **Parable of the Vineyard**, said, **"As man now is, God once was. As God now is, man may become."**

Heavenly Father is perfect in His sphere. He lives up to all the requirements and dictates of His level of progression. To be perfect—as our Father in Heaven is perfect—requires us to live up to all the requirements and dictates of our level of progression.

'What is she saying?' you may be thinking.

Well, I am saying this:

Let us compare the contents of a 3rd grade Math book to our level of progression, and let us compare the contents of a college-level Social Statistics book to Heavenly Father's level of perfection.

The 3rd grader is learning multiplication, division, measurement, simple graphing, etc. The Social Statistics student is learning hypothesis testing, bivariate measures, quantitative variations, computing of Z scores, A-novas, and chi-squares.

Throughout the learning process, we, as '3rd graders,' make mistakes. However, by the time we reach the next level, we should be able to add, subtract, multiply, divide, etc., without errors. In other words, we will be able to perform, on that level, with perfection.

The Social Statistics student will have no problems with adding, subtracting, multiplying, or dividing. That would be nothing more than a recreation to him or her. Their challenges and growth would be on a far more advanced level. Nonetheless, by the time they reach the next level, they too would be able to accomplish all that was taught in their Social Statistics course.

The 3rd-grade student is not expected to learn or do the same math, science, social studies, language arts, or any other subject or activity as the college student in order to reach perfection. Likewise, we, in our current mortal, fallible state, are not expected to be a God; said another way, we are not expected to do all Heavenly Father does as He does it.

President Joseph Fielding Smith said, **"I am seeking after my salvation, and I know that I can find it only in obedience to the laws of the Lord in keeping the commandments, in performing works of righteousness, following in the footsteps of our file leader, Jesus, the exemplar and the head of all."**

Like President Smith, we must conform our whole life, at every age, to the living of all the commandments, principles, precepts, doctrines, standards, and counsels, the way they have been given to us, without compromise, in every time, place and situation! Whether that be observance of the Sabbath, alignment with dress or dating standards, observance of the Word of Wisdom, tithing, temple attendance, the rendering of service, the quality of our speech, and our choice of entertainment, music, art, and recreation or any of all the other directives we have been given, we must live the gospel the way the Lord wrote it, with no revisions, addendums, or amendments, we must live the gospel just the way it is.

There are many voices in the world that will work effortlessly to pull you away from the truths that were delivered to us by the Lord and into the world, which is governed by the Adversary.

PLEASE! DO NOT FOLLOW SUCH COUNSEL!

You are worth so much more than any compromise, no matter how small, could ever possibly yield for you. You can do nothing that makes you more comfortable in the world that will not also make you more alien in the Kingdom of God.

To be perfect as our Father in Heaven is perfect is possible in this life because it means that we will obey all the commandments, observe and keep all the doctrines and counsels, live by all the precepts and standards to the very best of our abilities, without making exceptions, excuses or compromises, all the while, striving to be even better.

And, as we so do, we will share the most precious gift—the gospel—with others, both living and dead, through example, missionary work, family history and, temple work, and service.

In the name of Jesus Christ, Amen!

Taking Upon Yourself the Name of Jesus Christ

By

Eileen DiStasio-Clark

1992

Gaffney Ward in Gaffney, South Carolina

There are some basic needs which must be fulfilled to sustain life: food, water, shelter, and rest.

There are other needs which must be fulfilled to prolong life: health, fitness, and love.

There are three needs which must be fulfilled to enjoy life: reciprocal friendships, the acknowledgement, and acceptance of a person's existence and worth.

The nature of mortality requires us to give something for everything we need or want. In this life, we get nothing for nothing!

To obtain food, water, and shelter, we must exchange money with those who possess them. Even those who possess what we need had to exchange labor, time, and even some money to produce those commodities.

Health and fitness are purchased through the acquisition of adequate amounts of proper use and balance of the basic needs, as well as the expenditure of time and effort to exercise.

Love, which is essential to prolonging life and reciprocal friendships, acknowledgement of our existence, and acceptance of us as persons of worth are all purchased through service to others.

And, you are in complete control of how much of each of these you can purchase. That is determined by how much you serve.

There are several phrases which are received by many people as cleaver clichés, when in fact, they are anxious, self-evident truths.

1. If you want to be respected, be respectable.
2. If you want to be loved, be loveable.
3. To receive love, you must give love.
4. To have friends, you must be a friend.

These ideas, and others like them, are verifiable by service. And, because there are so many ways to serve, we can prove their truth multiple times throughout life. It would probably require a minimum of seven years of Sundays to discuss the myriad of ways we can serve. But there is one way, which may not immediately be recognized as a means of service. Yet, it is.

33

That way is to live, without compromise, the gospel doctrines and standards the way the Savior gave them to us! In **Mosiah 2: 17** King Benjamin teaches, **"When ye are in the <u>service</u> of your <u>fellow</u> beings, ye are only in the service of your God."**

In **Doctrine and Covenants 18: 21, 24, 25**, through revelation, Joseph Smith directed:

21. Take upon you the name of Christ, and speak the truth in soberness.

24. Wherefore, all men must take upon them the name which is given of the Father, for in that name shall they be called at the last day;

25. Wherefore, if they know not the name by which they are called, they cannot have place in the kingdom of my Father.

If you desire Exaltation in the Celestial Kingdom, then you must take upon yourself the name of Jesus Christ and live and serve as He would and as He did.

Several years ago, as part of our Home School Religion Class, to illustrate to my children what it means to take upon ourselves the name of Christ, I switched their identities for a day. Each child became someone else, and I recorded everything they did, whether favorable or unfavorable, under the other child's name. The next day, I read the list to them.

They were proud of all the favorable things associated with their names, even though they knew they had not done them, and frankly admitted that, but they were displeased with the unfavorable things associated with their names because they had not done those either. Now none of those unfavorable things were all that unfavorable. Still, they did not want anyone to think that they took too long to do a chore when they had not, or that they pouted for no particular reason when they had not pouted at all.

After reading the lists and listening to their responses, I told them what I had done and then explained to them that, in a similar way, that is what we do to Jesus with our every word, and action because, as Latter-Day Saints, when people look at us, in a way, they are seeing the Savior.

Because we profess to believe in His word, and we strive to become like Him, people will see in us 'what He is like' by the way we act and speak. Our appearances, words, actions, and attitudes, in essence, are associated with His name and teachings.

Since conclusion follows fact, and because we are to take upon ourselves the name of Jesus Christ, we must do the things that He has done and would do, speak the way He would speak, serve as He served, and live as He lived. That is the only way that we can 'purchase' exaltation. We serve Jesus and serve as He did, when we serve others the way He would.

Every child needs a father, a father who IS a father, not just the man in the house who brings home the money, gives orders, and expects his family to serve him. The Savior would not be that kind of a father.

A father who is doing his best to be like the Savior, would be a father who played with his children, helped support their mother, talked to them about their joys and problems, listened to them, really listened, not just heard them. He would take the time to see and understand their lives through their visions and perspectives. He would do all that he could so as to be able to really help them.

That would mean that he would strive to study, understand, and live the gospel the way that it is written, so that he could correlate its truths with the trials and stresses of family life He would love and serve them.

A mother needs to be there! To be home with and for her children, in every moment of joy, accomplishment, sorrow, and difficulty. She needs to be a support, a teacher, a friend. She needs to remember that her children are not her employees in the home, there just to cook and clean. Yes, they need to have chores so that they can learn to tend, and learn to be responsible, but a mother is the one who is there to care for them. She is the one who is to teach them those things by showing them what and how to do what needs to be done. It is also her responsibility to help, encourage, and support her husband.

Good parents will do all they can to help their children grow beyond their own limited beliefs in themselves to become what they truly are meant and able to be. And to do that, they must study and live the gospel the way it is written, without compromise, amendment, or exceptions. The gospel must be correlated with all experiences and challenges of life.

Now, because no one can teach that which they do not know, and because the gospel cannot be tailored to fit our lives. Our lives must be tailored to fit the gospel; parents must also study, learn, and live the gospel to its fullest. After all, children learn best through the examples of others, especially their parents. In fact, for all people of any age, how we look, speak, and act makes a big difference to others.

When we lived in Gaffney, South Carolina, we had a membership at the YMCA. On our second visit to the Y, we met the director. His attention was drawn to us by the number of children I have. The typical first question came, "You must run a daycare. Right?"

"No," I replied, "they are all my children by birth, and from only one marriage."

He then said, "You are Catholic. Right?"

I said, "No. I grew up Catholic, but when I was 19, I joined The Church of Jesus Christ of Latter-Day Saints."

Then he said, "Why would you do a thing like that?"

I replied, "When you find the truth, you can only accept it or reject it; you cannot change it. I chose to accept it and live by it."

He then told me that he had known some Mormons and was not impressed with them. He said they did not seem to be any different than anyone else and certainly no better.

My reply to that was this, "You just do not know the right kind of Mormons."

He then asked me, "What kind are you; the kind of Mormon who is what he is supposed to be or one who just says he is?"

I told him we always try very hard to do our best to be what we are supposed to be, without compromise.

He said, "Well, we'll see, won't we. We'll be watching you."

And they did! They watched how my kids treated each other, how they acted in public places, how they dressed, how they talked, how they responded to what I said. And they watched how I treated them and what I expected from them. They watched how I interacted with others. They took note of how we dressed and spoke, and… well, everything we were and did!

Now, Gaffney is a very small town. So, many of the people we had other associations with also attended the Y and conversations about us were exchanged between them—regularly!

People from the Pick-A-Flick video let others know that we never rented R, PG13, or most PG movies, no matter how popular or appealing those movies were said to be. In fact, Angie, the receptionist at Pick-A-Flick, had told them that she had never seen any of the kids even ask for one of those movies.

Our dentist was always asking questions. He became a close personal friend, so his questions were more specific than others. He would ask my girls about boyfriends and dating, clothing styles, and music choices, and always about our family. He was amazed by their responses.

His receptionist had said, "He is so impressed with your kids. Not only are they the most cooperative patients he has, he thinks your girls are the best teenagers he's ever known, and he has treated a lot of them, but he has never known any others who live by such high standards and do so willingly!"

When we told these people we were moving, some of them cried. They all asked us why and said they wanted us to stay.

When I talked to the YMCA director, he was disappointed that we were leaving, but he said that he would not even ask us to reconsider. He said, "You're the finest people I've known. I'm sure you are doing what you are doing because God told you to. I'm sorry to see you go, but glad to have known you, to have known Mormons who are what Mormons are supposed to be."

I know that my children had made a great impression on him. He had worked with youth for more than 30 years. He saw so many be pulled around, back and forth from one belief or lifestyle to another by whatever influence was the greatest. But my children never strayed from the high standards of the gospel, the way it is written.

The Ward that we had been in had many members who were true to the standards, but there were those who had not been. It was, sometimes, a sad experience because we were ostracized by some of those who did not adhere to the high standards as we did.

Once, I was asked by someone why we had to be so different. My reply was that we were not willing to compromise the way we lived the gospel. He thought I was hurting my children because I was keeping them from some of the activities that other kids were participating in. I told him that it was only the wrong ones that they did not join in on, and it was their choice, not just mine, not to do so.

I knew that it had been difficult for my children; it had been difficult for me as well. But then, one day, we received a phone call from one of the young boys in the ward that made all the difference.

This young boy was feeling rather depressed and needed someone to talk to. He called my oldest daughter because he trusted her more than he trusted anyone else. In the course of their half-hour conversation, he said to her, "I am so glad you stand up for what you know is right. I think that is neat!"

Then, the night before we left Gaffney, my girls were honored with a cake and were acknowledged at a Young Women's activity. For almost an hour after the meeting, the girls were hugged by crying friends who did not want them to leave. This surprised all of us, but I later realized, it because of the words spoken by the young man who had previously called my daughter. He told me that they, the youth, had begun to find strength in the standards because my daughters had refused to compromise them.

When he asked me why we had to leave, I told him that it was because that was what Heavenly Father directed us to do. He replied with, "That is so sad; who will we look up to now?"

While our time there had been filled with both good experiences and difficult times, there was much good and learning that came from it. All of that can be summed up like this:

To serve others well:

1. Listen to the hearts of others
2. Remember their Birthdays, Special Days, and Just Days
3. Visit others simply because they live
4. Give what you have to others: gifts, treats, but mostly your time, your praise for the good that is in them, your love, with no thought of return or thanks—just because you have it to give.
5. Sacrifice for the benefit of others

But also remember to:

1. Serve your family first
2. Serve others as needed
3. Focus not on serving yourself

...and you will be serving Heavenly Father.

Most importantly, remember that you will be serving exquisitely if you serve by taking upon yourselves the name of Jesus the Christ, and by living the gospel as it is written, without compromise.

In the name of Jesus Christ, Amen!

I Will… Because I Love Him

By

Eileen DiStasio-Clark

Around 1994

Blue Springs 2nd Ward in Blue Springs, Missouri

April 28, 1973, was a landmark day in my life; it was the day I was baptized into The Church of Jesus Christ of Latter-Day Saints. My life and character were to be transformed gradually and in a way, I would not have imagined.

Things I had always believed but had never been taught, e.g., the eternity of life and destiny and the identity of the "companion" I had often felt and to whom I had spoken on occasion, finally found an answer and enlightenment. Choice of paths became clearer, and reasons for choice were predefined.

From birth, I have hungered for and feasted upon that which is spiritual. Preeminent in my life has been the desire to know and please my Father in Heaven. Through the gospel of Jesus Christ, I have found continual fulfillment for all the worthwhile desires of life and the impregnable, impermeable bond for my family, the most precious of all the jewels of eternity with which I could be endowed.

Accepting the gospel meant sacrificing many things. Throughout my life, my father and I had been closer than

43

crossed fingers. Never had I done anything that would have made him unhappy or caused him disappointment. At 19, and for the first time in my life, I found myself in a position in which I had to choose between my father's wishes and the "desires of my heart."

Upon his learning of my interest in Mormons, he issued the warning, "If you ever consider joining them, you will not have my blessings."

To me, that was like saying I would not be his daughter. I did not want that to happen. I did not want to hurt or anger my father, but I knew I was being urged and prompted by the Spirit. Indecision led me to the scriptures, where I found my answer in **Matthew 17: 37: "He that <u>loveth</u> father or mother <u>more</u> than me is not worthy of me: and he that <u>loveth</u> son or daughter more than me is not worthy of me."**

I had ALWAYS loved God and would not, for anyone or any reason, hurt, deny, or disappoint Him. I chose the gospel and baptism, sacrificing the relationship I had held with my father. The many months that followed were adorned with sadness and tears as my father kept his word. But, in time, the Lord's time, my reward was the baptisms of all of my family members and an even more enhanced relationship with my father than I had had before, something I never thought could be possible!

In all of the many years that have followed, there have been multitudes of other sacrifices, challenges, burdens, and trials. But uncompromising adherence to the gospel doctrines, precepts, and standards has always brought the rewards of blessings, comfort, wisdom, greater knowledge, understanding, and most precious of all, ever-increasing testimony.

I know, as surely as I know of my own existence, that Heavenly Father is our God, that Jesus the Christ is His son, our Savior, that the Holy Spirit is a living member of the Godhead and my constant companion, that the gospel, as taught by The Church of Jesus Christ of Latter-Day Saints, is the true word of God and all that has been revealed to man thus-far, and that The Church of Jesus Christ of Latter-Day Saints is the Kingdom of God on the earth with Jesus, our Lord, at the head of it. I know, with equal surety, that President Howard W. Hunter is the only true prophet of God on the earth today, and that he speaks for the Lord as a man speaketh for himself.

I know, also, that Lucifer is authentic. He is a fallen angel, Satan, the devil, and his powers are greater than man's, except that man calls upon the Lord to be his protector and shield against the Adversary.

On a glistening July morning, while driving home to Blue Springs, Missouri, from Lawrence, Kansas, I was reminded of the singular position true saints hold in this world.

Several years ago, I committed myself to observing the speed limits wherever I drive. In so doing, I noted, on several occasions, but particularly on that morning, driving so much of the highway at a time when traffic was not congested that those drivers who exceed the speed limit, thereby putting themselves outside the law, drive in the company of others, usually many others. Those drivers who observe the speed limit, thereby remaining within the law, drive alone, or, at best, in the company of just a few.

As I approached a segment of the roadway that was under construction, the traffic bottlenecked, and I found myself in the company of everyone. With less than a quarter of a car-length between us, there was no visibility beyond my own vehicle and those immediately surrounding me. To know where to go, I had to follow the drivers ahead of me and hope they were going where I wanted and needed to go.

A large tractor-trailer obstructed my view of the signs I needed to see, and, to my dismay, I found myself in the wrong lane and headed in the wrong direction. I had to travel many miles out of my way to find another road leading to my destination or end up in the wrong place, a place where I did not want to be. I was annoyed with myself because I had driven that route several times before and thought I knew how to get home. I did not believe I should have made such a stupid mistake.

A few days later, driving the same route, that time with an unobstructed view, I once again found myself in the wrong lane, headed for the wrong place. That time, I erred because I was looking for the wrong signs.

As I pondered on these experiences, the Spirit drew an analogy for me, from which to learn.

In life, those who live outside the law of the gospel do so in the company of others, oftentimes, many others. Theirs may be the lives filled with friends, fame, popularity, and perhaps wealth, which many see as blessings and glories of this world.

Those who live within the law of the gospel, do so, very often, alone, or, at best, in the company of just a few. But theirs are the lives endowed with happiness, contentment, the love of God, progression, and understanding, which are the divine blessings of eternity.

When traveling in the company of the world, as in the bottleneck of congested traffic, it becomes difficult to see the signs of our Lord and Savior. We must trust in others to get us where we need to go. However, when we follow the wrong others, cannot see the signs of the gospel, or look for the wrong signs, we will, undoubtedly, end up going in the wrong direction. It then will be necessary to travel the many extra miles of repentance to get back on the right road, or we will end up in the wrong place, a place we did not want to go.

It is my testimony that it is better for us to travel alone on the right road, the road which leads to a Celestial reward than it is to travel in the company of others on the wrong road, the road which leads to anything else.

Though I may be labeled extreme, self-righteous, ridiculous, silly... I have committed myself to living the gospel, as it is written, without compromise, because I know that to be the best and only way to eternal life, with my family in the Celestial and Exalted Kingdom of my Father in Heaven.

Weak and imperfect as I consider myself to be, I know I can gain the noblest blessings of my Heavenly Father because He said I could.

Overwhelming and cumbersome as the challenge of mortality is, I know I can rise above it and overcome myself because He said I could.

Unworthy and lowly as I am sure that I am, I know He will help me because he said He would.

Rough and imperfect as mortality makes us, I know he will refine me because He said He would.

Though small as a speck in the universe, only one of the countless numbers of His children, I know He loves me because He said He does.

So, alone or with others, I will live the gospel, as it is written, without compromise, defend my Father in Heaven and Jesus, my Savior, stand for the right in all things, in all places, and obey, teach, and serve whatever, wherever, whenever, and whomever He should require of me, because I love Him.

In the name of Jesus Christ, Amen!

A July Thought

By

Eileen DiStasio-Clark

Around 2000

Blue Springs 2nd Ward in Blue Springs, Missouri

Out of the 6,015,541,237 people who populate this world, only 273,617,988 live in the United States of America. How do you suppose you ended up as one of them? You were born here? You—or your family—chose to emigrate here? Well, whatever your answer, hold that thought while you consider this!

In **I Nephi 2:2,** Nephi says, **And it came to pass that the Lord commanded my father, even in a dream, that he should take his family and depart into the wilderness.**

In **I Nephi 17:13,** the Lord says, **And I will also be your light in the wilderness; and I will prepare the way before you, if it so be that ye shall keep my commandments; wherefore, inasmuch as ye shall keep my commandments ye shall be led toward the promised land; and ye shall know that it is by me that ye are led.**

Lehi brought his family to America, not because it was a good idea. He did not say, "Ok, kids, we need a change; let us go to the promised land." Nor did they come for work. He did not suggest, "Boys, there are not enough good jobs in

Jerusalem; let us move to a new land." He came because the Lord so directed!

Christopher Columbus and the pilgrims came because the Lord directed them. In **I Nephi 13: 12, 13,** Nephi teaches, **And I looked and beheld a man among the Gentiles, who was separated from the seed of my brethren by the many waters; and I beheld the Spirit of God, that it came down and wrought upon the man; and he went forth upon the many waters, even unto the seed of my brethren, who were in the promised land. And it came to pass that I beheld the Spirit of God, that it wrought upon other Gentiles; and they went forth out of captivity, upon many waters.**

My great-grandpa Pellicciotti brought his family to America because he felt it was the right thing to do. He could not explain the feeling; he just knew he had to come. My grandpa DeStasio came to America because he knew God wanted him here. May I suggest that Heavenly Father has directed the emigration of many people because this is the land in which He wanted them?

Now, for those of us who were born here—did that just happen?

Well, biologically, I suppose it did, but the body is only the tabernacle for the spirit.

Who decided where that spirit was going to be sent?

Heavenly Father did!!

He could have sent your spirit to a body in Italy, China, Tasmania, Sri Lanka, or any other nation, but he sent you here. Therefore, I would like to further suggest that each of us is here, in America, because this is where Heavenly Father wants us to be. With this assignment comes privilege and responsibility.

The privileges are many and obvious. If you study the cultures of the world, these privileges become even more pronounced. The right to vote on legislation is NOT a universal privilege. Our constitution allows us this privilege. Do you exercise it?

With the privilege of having a voice in the government comes the responsibility to use it. If you do not, then you must accept what others—those who do exercise that right—choose for you. In simple words, for the child in us, if Mom says, "Ok guys, you have three choices for breakfast: pancakes, eggs, or cereal," and your brothers and sisters choose eggs, but you, who said nothing because you were occupied with Saturday morning cartoons, wanted cereal; you will get eggs.

The Fourth Article of the Bill of Rights gives us the right to bear arms for our own protection. I used to think—when I was really young... REALLY YOUNG ...that bearing arms meant we did not have to wear sleeves. I did not know how that would protect us. Later, when I was still young, my dad took my brother and me target shooting on Saturday mornings, and I learned its meaning and that not everyone had that right.

We learned to shoot a German Mouser that Dad had brought home from the Second World War. He told us stories about the war, the prisoners he guarded, and things they would tell him about their countries. I began then to see that we were much more privileged than some others.

The number of our privileges is far too great to list completely. They include everything from speaking openly of our views and beliefs to worshiping as we choose, to selecting our own dates and spouses, to choosing our occupation, to having the number of children we desire and raising them according to the dictates and tenants of our beliefs and characters, to… the list goes on and on.

Many of our rights are being challenged today, and that makes it essential that we exercise our responsibility to become and remain active in our governmental process. Now, you may think that Heavenly Father will always protect this nation and our freedoms. That may be true, but He will work through righteous men to do this, and there is a condition prescribed to it!

If you will recall, the Lord, when speaking to Nephi said, **"…if you keep my commandments!"** By Heavenly Father's choice, we are privileged to be Americans. Because we have been given that privilege, we have the responsibility to keep the commandments—ALL of them!

Do we really observe the Sabbath Day—ALL DAY? Do we use the entire day to serve the Lord, study His word, and perform His labors? Or do we merely attend our meetings, then spend the balance of the day watching T.V., playing or watching a sporting event, going out to eat, attending a party, shopping, or…?

Do we honestly obey the Word of Wisdom—by the spirit— as pertaining to our habits of food and drink, and rest and exercise, or just by the letter, only refraining from those substances specifically stated in the verses of **Doctrine and Covenants 89**?

Do we diligently strive to learn and live by all the commandments, principles, and councils of the gospel and follow the prophets and apostles, or do we choose what we want to live, what is easy or convenient, and hide from or ignore the rest, perhaps pretending we do not know better?

Make our choices in entertainment, clothing, behavior, and attitude represent us as children of God, the Father of all righteousness, or do they identify us as agents of Lucifer?

Do we serve others? Do we support our leaders?

These are the last days! These are the days in which the Lord's elect could be deceived.

How? I wondered this for a long time, but I think I now know.

Of my eleven children, the first eight had been baptized on their birthdays. This was a family tradition, and traditions, especially family traditions, are important to me. I wanted all of my children to be baptized on their birthdays. Ergo, my ninth child was to be baptized in the month of July. We had chosen the pattern and material for her dress, and planned the program. Then, I was told she could not be baptized until August because all children's baptisms had to be performed on the Saturday preceding the first Sunday of the month. I was not happy! It did not seem fair. What difference does it make on what day a child is baptized?

My bishop, being sensitive and thoughtful, showed me the letter of instruction he had received. Because the direction came from the Lord, as do all the councils, instructions, and advice we receive from the prophets and apostles, I willingly accepted it. However, I cannot tell this story without admitting that I felt the temptation to complain against my leaders, knowing that somewhere, some time, there would be exceptions to this rule. But I did not do that!

I wanted, and want, to obey the Lord in everything—large and small—and therein lies the strength or the weakness. Indeed, what difference does it make what day a child is baptized? What is important is not the day, but the ordinance.

For me, what was important was not the day of the baptism, but the test.

Was I willing to follow the Lord, through His leaders, in the small things as well as the large? Would I let the influence of Satan cause me to see boulders where there were barely pebbles?

When we begin to question, contradict, or argue with our leaders, when the small things become big things to us, when we put our desires and personal choices before the words of the Lord, we need to remember this: **Doctrine & Covenants 1: 38: "...whether by mine own voice or by the voice of my servants, it is the same."** When we choose to limit our learning in hopes of not being accountable for that principle, we hand to Satan the key to our soul.

Now, Side but Important Note: I did happily, and with gratitude for the Lord's teaching, conform to the new standard for Children's Baptisms.

Let us all, always ponder the privilege we have of living in this noble, chosen land of freedom and choice, consider the rights and responsibilities that come with that privilege, and understand that we bear an obligation to live righteously, or we will forever forfeit all the blessings and privileges of an even more noble and chosen kingdom of honor, privilege, and glory.

In the name of Jesus Christ, Amen!

Correct Knowledge

By

Eileen DiStasio-Clark

Around 2007

Platte City Ward in Platte City, Missouri

In a court of law, a testimony is a statement used for evidence or proof. As part of both the defense and the prosecution, testimony is presented, evaluated, and weighed to formulate a verdict.

Verdicts are to be rendered when there is evidence sufficient to prove beyond a reasonable doubt, not beyond all doubt, for that is not possible. Unless a person who has experienced or eye-witnessed an occurrence, there is always a place to wonder.

So, the law requires only the satisfaction of reasonable doubt. Or, in other words, the juror can honestly say to himself, "Well, I suppose there is some possibility that he or she could be guilty or innocent, as the case may be, but I see nothing to suggest that such could be true. A verdict rendered upon this type of conviction is sufficient for execution or release.

In the academic world, one of the most common and misused ideologies is that of thinking outside the box. It is supposed to suggest an addition to spiritual/religious knowledge through the scientific process. However, in reality, you are not being asked to think outside the box. You are being asked to think inside a different box—the box of mortal philosophies.

You see, scientists do not seek to prove anything; they seek to disprove! In the scientific process:

1. A hypothesis is formed to disprove a standing theory
2. Tests are devised to prove the hypothesis, which would disprove the theory
3. Only after hundreds of failures to disprove the theory, is it accepted, 'tentatively', as fact, with the understanding that, at some point, someone may yet discover curious evidence to challenge it. Until that time, we are expected to accept scientific facts as proof and theories as evidence.

Facts and theories are testimonies of science and academics.

Disprovable facts, uncertain theories, and the satisfaction of reasonable doubt are as close as we get to the truth when we rely upon the academics of man to find it. And what does that leave us with?

1. Questions unanswered
2. Purposes undiscovered
3. Joys unattained

All of these things we are told come from man's research efforts, not an adherence to a belief in God. Yet, those with a testimony of God, and particularly those of us blessed with a knowledge and testimony of the correct and complete gospel have:

Answers, and a true source of answers to our questions

Meaning and direction for our lives because we know its purpose

True happiness, even through our sorrows, because we know that everything in our lives can be used for our ultimate achievement, which is Exaltation

But, of course, even for those who believe in God, only a testimony, nourished and lived by, will produce these results.

To possess a knowledge of the gospel is not enough! You must have a testimony of its truthfulness and validity of your own!

We have the testimonies of others:

Isaiah said in chapter **6,** verse 5 …**mine eyes have seen the King, the LORD of hosts.**

Nephi in **2Nephi** chapter **11** verse **2** said **And now I, Nephi, write <u>more</u> of the words of <u>Isaiah</u>, for my soul delighteth in his words. For I will liken his words unto my people, and I will send them forth unto all my children, for he**

verily <u>saw</u> my <u>Redeemer</u>, even as I have seen him.

The apostles, Mark, Matthew, Luke, and John gave us books

of

Testimony, theirs and those of others

Joesph Smith gave us an account of his visions

Many, many people have shared their testimonies

Now, you may believe that they believe what they are telling you, but you will never believe what they are telling you if you do not have your own testimony. And, each one cf us must gain that for ourselves.

Elder Heber C. Kimball once said: **"Let me say to you, that many of you will see the time when you will have all the trouble, trial and persecution that you can stand, and plenty of opportunities to show that you are true to God and his work. This Church has before it many close places through which it will have to pass before the work of God is crowned with victory.**

"The time will come when no man nor woman will be able to endure on borrowed light. Each will have to be guided by the light within himself. If you do not have it, how can you stand?" (Orson F. Whitney, *Life of Heber C. Kimball,* 3d. ed.)

Though we possess the Light of Christ, which is knowledge brought with us from Pre-Earth Live, which is not completely shielded but only veiled, a testimony does not just happen! It is the product of faith, tried and tested, tested and proved!

In **Ether 12:6** we read: **And now, I, Moroni, would speak somewhat concerning these things; I would show unto the world that <u>faith</u> is things which are <u>hoped</u> for and <u>not</u> seen; wherefore, dispute not because ye see not, for ye receive no witness until after the <u>trial</u> of your faith.**

Our faith is tried and tested through challenges and suffering. When you feel good, it is not difficult to be good. But when you are lonely, angry, diffident, when you are mocked, neglected, hurt, when you are ill, in pain, and mistreated, do you trust God? Do you still live according to gospel principles and precepts, or do you give up to justify a wrong-doing, a compromise of principle? Do you succumb to temptation?

If you remain true to the promise and choice you made before coming to Earth, upon your baptism, and every Sunday at Sacrament Meeting, your testimony will be increased. Righteous living is a requirement!

In **John 7:17** the Lord said: **If any man will <u>do</u> his <u>will</u>, he shall <u>know</u> of the doctrine, whether it be of God, or whether I speak of myself.**

This is both a condition: we must obey His law and a promise that we will receive a testimony.

61

President David O. McKay said: **"A testimony of the gospel of Jesus Christ is the most sacred, the most precious gift in our lives, obtained only by adherence to the principles of the gospel, not by following the paths of the world."**

Why? Why do we have to be good first, then get the testimony? Why does the Lord not just visit us and tell us all this is true and worthwhile?

Well, at least one reason is this: it is because it is human nature to be skeptical! For most things, almost all people want proof. "Show me!" people say. "Prove it!" Essentially, they put themselves above God. But that is faulty!

Heavenly Father does not have to prove anything to us, but He will reveal all truth to those who prepare themselves spiritually, humble themselves, and turn to Him, with sincere desire, ready to receive the truth.

President Joseph Fielding Smith said in a 1903 Conference Talk: **[A testimony] comes to us …because we put ourselves in harmony with the principle of communication from God to man. We believe, we repent of and confess our sins, we do that which the Lord requires in order to gain a remission of our sins, and thus we receive the gift of the Holy Spirit.**

In the name of Jesus Christ, Amen!

Spiritual Preparedness

By

Eileen DiStasio-Clark

Around 2009

Platte Woods Ward in Kansas City, Missouri

"'Picture with me in your mind's eye, if you will, a church building with a recently-placed sign reading, 'Spiritual Fuel Available—No Rationing—No Stamps—No Quotas—Come and Prepare.' 'Picture with me further a home with a welcome mat bearing the inscription, 'Welcome Neighbor—Spiritual Oil Available—Come In As You Are.' 'Picture with me still further an individual whose very countenance radiates, 'I know God lives—my cup runneth over.'"

These were the words of Marvin J. Ashton in the April 1974 General Conference, almost 35 years ago—a time of fuel shortages and gas rationings. He entitled his talk, "A Time of Urgency," and he said: "Brethren and sisters, we are living in a time of urgency. We are living in a time of spiritual crisis. We are living in a time close to midnight."

Thirty-five years ago, Elder Ashton said we were close to midnight. Midnight is referenced as the time of the Savior's return. In Matthew 25:6, in the Parable of the Ten Virgins, we read: And at midnight there was a cry made, Behold, the bridegroom cometh; go ye out to meet him.

How do we know this references the time of the Second Coming?

Doctrine and Covenants 45: 56 explains: And at that day, when I shall come in my **glory**, shall the parable be fulfilled which I spake concerning the ten **virgins.**

So, if we were close to midnight 35 years ago, where are we now?

Would you say our time for preparation is passing? I believe I would!

So, how then can we be sure we are prepared, or how can we get prepared?

You do know this is something each of us must do for ourselves. Yes?

Listen again to Elder Ashton: "The responsibility for having oil in our personal lamps is an individual requirement and opportunity. The oil of spiritual preparedness cannot be shared."

Parents cannot provide oil for their children's lamps. Husbands cannot provide oil for their wives' lamps, nor wives for their husbands'. Brothers and sisters too, must purchase their own oil.

Why?

Well think of it this way.

Mommy is hungry; so are her sons and daughters. She makes a nice lunch for all of them, but only she eats it. The children will still be hungry. Even if Mommy eats all that has been prepared, the children will still be hungry.

Suppose Daddy is tired; so are the kids. The kids go to bed early and get plenty of rest, but Daddy does not go to bed—at least not early—and does not get the rest he needs. All the rest the kids got will not help Daddy feel better.

And so, it is with Spiritual Preparation. Mom's scripture study will not help her teenage children understand the word of the Lord. She may share her knowledge, but she cannot do her children's learning.

To be spiritually prepared for the quakes and tremors Satan initiates in our lives, we must strengthen our own faith, experience our own sincere repentance, and exercise our own obedience! No one can do that for us. Others may help, but we must initiate and follow through with our own preparedness. Elder Henry B. Eyring, in the October 2005 Conference, said, "It will take unshakable faith in the Lord, Jesus Christ, to choose the way to eternal life."

To have faith in Jesus Christ, you must know Him!

If I told you I could lay wood flooring, put in a new kitchen—sink, stove, cabinets, everything—take down walls, rewire the electric… would you hire me to remodel your house?

Maybe you would, if you trusted my word, but could you trust my word if you did not know me?

But to know how truthful or capable I am, you would need to get to know me. You would need to talk to me and listen to what I say. You would need to see what I have done, maybe even watch me work!

To know the Savior well enough to know that you can trust Him, you have to talk to Him—through prayer. You have to listen to Him—in meditation and pondering. You have to see what He has done—through a deep and deliberate study of the scriptures. And, you have to watch Him, by serving others and getting close enough to Him to see and recognize the blessings in their lives and the blessings in your own.

When you know Him that well, you can develop the type of faith that works for you.

Elder Eyring said: "It is by using that faith we can know the will of God. And it is by exercising that faith in Jesus Christ that we can resist temptation and gain forgiveness through the atonement."

Faith brings us to repentance, which is the second significant step in preparation. Repentance is not a simple, "Oops, I did not mean that' I am sorry." It is not regretful because you "got caught". It is, as defined in the Bible Dictionary: ...a change of mind, i.e., a fresh view about God, about oneself, and about the world. Since we are born into conditions of mortality, repentance comes to mean a turning of the heart and will to God, and a renunciation of sin to which we are naturally inclined. Without this, there can be no progress in the things of the soul's salvation, for all accountable persons are tainted by sin and must be cleansed in order to enter the Kingdom of Heaven. Repentance is not optional for salvation; it is a commandment of God.

Once you have this foundation built, you must secure it with obedience to all of the Lord's commandments, precepts, and counsels because they all matter!

It is not enough to pay a full tithe if your entertainment choices would invite the Spirit to leave you. It is not enough to honor the Sabbath and live the Word of Wisdom, if the Lord would have to "close His eyes" to look at you because your clothing is immodest and unwholesome.

Obedience to all the Lord's commandments and counsels is absolutely essential!

And not just for today or this week, a few months, or a couple of years, but for our full life—to the end!! We must endure to the end!!!

To strengthen a home against an earthquake, the house has to be bolted to the foundation, the cripple walls need to be reinforced, and the materials used in the foundation and cripple walls must not be faulty!

To strengthen ourselves against the quakes and tremors of Satan—to be spiritually prepared—we must lay our foundation with perfect materials, which are implicit faith, sincere repentance, and an abiding obedience to the commandments and counsels of the gospel.

Then we must bolt ourselves to that foundation with President Monson's Formula for Success: "...first, search the scriptures with diligence; second plan your life with purpose, third, teach the truth with testimony, and fourth, serve the Lord with love."

Finally, we must reinforce our cripple walls with only the purest principles of the gospel, replacing any faulty ideas of man. By doing these things, we will stand when the world falls!

In the name of Jesus Christ, Amen!

My Body is a Temple

By

Eileen DiStasio-Clark and Aubrey Johnson

Around 2009

Platte Woods Ward in Kansas City, Missouri

A temple is a holy place. It is considered the House of the Lord and the most sacred place on earth. In temples, we make sacred covenants with Heavenly Father that make it possible for us to go home and live with Him after we leave this earth. Because the temple is so sacred, Heavenly Father wants us to respect and honor it by doing what is right so that we will be worthy to enter it. He also expects us to keep it clean on the inside and outside. Since cleanliness is next to Godliness, keeping the temple clean and beautiful helps us remember our Heavenly Father and feel close to Him when we are there.

Our bodies are sacred too. **Elder L. Tom Perry** said, **"The Lord sets a high standard for us in telling us to consider our bodies a temple."** Just as a temple is the House of the Lord, our body is a temple for our spirits, but it is only holy if we make it holy. We must take care of our bodies by obeying the Word of Wisdom. That means we will eat healthy foods and not use tobacco, drink alcohol, or take any drugs. We should only take the medicine that we need when we need it. It also means that we will get enough exercise and sleep. If we do not do these things, if we put bad things into our bodies, it is like lighting a campfire inside the house; it will cause a lot of damage.

We must also take care of our minds. **Elder L. Tom Perry** said, **"Mental health is also important and should not be overlooked, as it can affect us both physically and spiritually."** To take care of our minds we must choose music, movies, books, games, and other stuff that are good and will help us feel closer to Heavenly Father. He does not want us to fill our minds with things that are not good and wholesome because if we do, we will not have the Spirit with us and, like a GPS that is not working properly, they will take us in the wrong direction, away from Him.

We also need to keep our bodies clean on the outside. We have been instructed to not get tattoos and body piercings but to dress modestly and take good care of our natural beauty. **President Gordon B. Hinckley** said, **"A tattoo is a graffiti on the temple of the body."** How we look on the outside is one of the first things that tells others what we are on the inside, so we must take care of our appearance, just as the Lord has us take care of His temples.

If we think of our bodies as temples and we respect temples as Holy Houses of God, we will be motivated to take good care of our bodies so that we can be worthy to enter the House of the Lord and return home to Heavenly Father when we are done here.

In the name of Jesus Christ, Amen!

Making Room for Christ in Your Life

By

Eileen DiStasio-Clark

January 2016

Platte Woods Ward in Kansas City, Missouri

Micah was excited! So excited, in fact, that he did not even mind that his room would no longer be his room. Grandpa was coming to stay with them, and he was going to sleep in Micah's room. Micah would share a room with his baby brother.

He did not mind that his toys would have to go to the Family Room or that his clothes would be stuffed into half a closet. He loved Grandpa more than the Man-in-the-Moon loved cheese. Nothing was too much to give up for Grandpa.

So happy was he to have Grandpa coming to live with them that he volunteered to help Mommy clean his room, repaint the walls, and put up new curtains. "After all," he thought aloud, "Grandpa is worth it!"

What would we be willing to do or give up if Grandpa were coming to stay with us? Would he be worth any sacrifice? Would Christ be worth any sacrifice? Would we clean our rooms, paint our walls, and put up new curtains for Him?

Making room for Christ in our lives is as simple as making room for Grandpa—or as hard—depending upon our love for Him.

We need to pray and study the scriptures daily, attend church meetings, fast, pay our tithing and offerings, align our lives with the gospel's principles, and do all else that the Lord requires of us. We know this, but....

Would we give up our room? Or, in other words, would we give up what we want, maybe what we have, to do whatever the Lord asks of us? Or, would we be more inclined to tell the Lord what we want Him to give to us?

The apostle, Matthew, gave up his room. He was a Publican, or tax collector, and was required to pay a fixed amount of money to the Roman government each year. Publicans were free to collect as much as they could and most of them were corrupt and detested, but Matthew was different.

As recorded in the Testament of **Luke 5: 27, 28,** we learn that **"...He** [meaning Christ] **went forth, and saw a Publican named Levi,** [that is Matthew] **sitting at the receipt of custom: and he said unto him, "Follow me."**

And he left all, rose up, and followed Him."

Matthew did not ask the Lord to wait until he was done counting his money. He did not accept His invitation with conditions; that is to say, he did not ask Christ, "What is in it for me?" He simply followed. Do we?

When the Lord asks us to pay our tithing and fast offering, do we check our bank account and review our bills first to see if we can afford it, or do we just pay it?

When He builds temples for us to attend, do we go, or are we too busy?

When He provides standards for dress and grooming, entertainment, and behavior, do we comply, or do we modify?

Do we need to ask ourselves, "Would I give up my room for Jesus?"

Would we share our room with a brother or sister? That is to say, would we give of ourselves for the benefit of another?

The unnamed Samaritan shared his room. If you recall the story from **Luke 10**, not only did he stop to help the injured Jew, but also, as recorded in verses **33-35**, he gave of his time and substance to render that help.

33. ...a certain Samaritan... had compassion on him.

34. And went to him, and bound up his wounds, pouring in oil and wine, and set him on his own beast, and brought him to an inn, and took care of him.

35. And on the morrow when he departed, he took out two pence, and gave them to the host, and said unto him,

take care of him; and whatsoever thou spendest more, when I come again, I will repay thee."

The Samaritan did not do as the priest and the Levite had done, ignore him and just walk on; he stopped to help him. Would we?

The Lord has constructed means by which we can share our time, means, and resources. He calls them Home Teaching, Visiting Teaching, church callings, and compassionate service.

Do we do it? Or do we put our time and efforts into working overtime, neglecting family and gospel responsibilities so we can get all those things we do not need?

Should we ask ourselves, "Would I share my room with Jesus?"

Would we put our toys in the family room and stuff our clothes in half a closet? Said another way, would we redirect our focus and maintain a humble perspective?

St. Francis of Assisi, as a youth, was a member of a rowdy, violent gang, partying immorally and committing crimes. However, he found his faith when he spent a year in jail, living with the rats and the lepers. At the age of 25, Francis renounced all claims on his family's wealth and social standing and spent the rest of his life focused on the Lord's work.

On what are we focused—the house that exceeds our needs, with trophies on the mantle and too many cars in the garage, on the temporal gains and applause, or on the means to bring comfort to those who struggle, and provision to those who lack?

Benjamin was a king; he ruled over the Nephites, but he lived as one of them. In the book of **Mosiah 2: 12, 14**, we read:

12. I say unto you that as I have been suffered to <u>spend</u> my days in your service, even up to this time, and have not sought <u>gold</u> nor silver nor any manner of riches of you;

14. And even I, myself, have <u>labored</u> with mine own <u>hands</u> that I might serve you, and that ye should not be <u>laden</u> with taxes, and that there should nothing come upon you which was grievous to be borne

Are we like Benjamin? Do we give of ourselves what we expect of others? Do we exhibit the right behaviors that teach others how to perform? Or do we talk the talk, but not walk the walk?

Do we need to ask ourselves, am I focused on the work of the Lord; do I stuff my clothes in half of Jesus' closet, or do I fill up all of my own?

Would we clean the room for Jesus and repaint the walls? That is, will we remove the dirt of sin from our lives and not return to play in it again?

From the book, **"Mafia to Mormon: My Conversion Story",** we learn that **Mario Facione** was a prosperous mafia boss until his wife opened the door to the missionaries. Through a long and interesting process, he gained a testimony, and he was baptized, but he had not given up his business until his bishop told him that he could not serve two masters; he had to choose one and let go of the other. It took Mario a bit of time and a lot of prayer to determine what he would do. He told his bishop . . .

"'Look, if I walk away from this and tell them I want out, they'll kill me.' 'Guys don't walk away from this.'

"He sat there, looked at me and began shaking his head. **"Don't you have any faith?"** he asked.

"Well, yeah," I responded. **"But you don't know my circumstances."**

He paused briefly. **"There's nothing in your circumstances that you have to worry about,"** he said, as I sat in disbelief. **"So what if you get killed."**

"I knew what he meant. That would only bring me a step closer to a reunion with my Heavenly Father and Jesus Christ. Still, it was one I was reluctant to take just yet.

"But I haven't had a chance to get into the temple yet," I said back to him.

"You can only serve on master," he repeated**."**

Mario did leave the mafia, losing his temporal comforts, but he kept his life, his testimony, and his word to God.

When we met him about 10 ½ years ago, he was a humble truck driver, working hard to make enough to sustain himself and his wife, but he was also a worker in the Detroit Temple.

Every day we wash dirt off our bodies and out of our hair. Do we wash the dirt of sin from our souls with equal diligence, or do we excuse ourselves of the so-called 'little things,' only repenting within our comfort zone or when it is time for a temple-recommended interview?

Will we clean our room for Jesus—using the soap of the atonement that He gave us—and keep it clean?

Would we hang new curtains? That is, would we shelter ourselves from the temptations of the Adversary and the world and bask in the light of Christ?

What are the safety settings on our internet? What is the rating limit of the movies we permit ourselves to view? What is the content of the materials we read, the music to which we listen, the conversations in which we take part, and the environments in which we socialize?

Do we need to ask ourselves, will I hang up Jesus' curtains?

Making room for Jesus in our lives requires only that we do what we said we would do—live His gospel, as He gave it to us, without compromise or revision.

When did we say that?

In the Pre-Earth Life, when we chose to follow the Father's Plan and again, in this life when we were baptized.

Just as Mario's bishop told him, we cannot serve two masters. If we do not make room for Christ in our lives, we will find Satan sitting by our side.

You see, we have to make room for Christ, open the door, and invite Him in because, although He will always do all that He can to be with us, He will not impose upon us. We were given our agency—the freedom to make our own choices—He will always respect that.

Satan, on the other hand, who wanted to take away that agency, will not respect it. Like it or not, Satan will invite himself into our lives, barge through the door, and take over.

The best, the only way to keep him out, is to make room for Christ, invite Him to be our guest and hire Him as our security guard.

I share these thoughts with you in the name of Jesus Christ,
Amen!

Let the Holy Spirit Be Your Guide

By

Eileen DiStasio-Clark

June 17, 2018

Platte Woods Ward in Kansas City, Missouri

In **Doctrine and Covenant 45: 57,** we read: **For they that are wise and have received the <u>truth</u>, and have taken the Holy Spirit for their <u>guide</u>, and have not been deceived—verily I say unto you, they shall not be hewn down and cast into the <u>fire</u>, but shall abide the day.**

In his Conference Talk this April (2018), **Elder Larry Y. Wilson** of the Seventy said, **"It is an extraordinary privilege to "have …the Holy Spirit for [our] guide."** Why? What does that mean?

The **Merriam-Webster** and **The King James Bible Dictionaries** tell us that a guide is someone who: **Leads or directs us, Exhibits and Explains things, Directs someone's conduct or course of life; like a mentor, or is a member of a group, like a workforce or a class, a club, any organized body of people, on whom the actions of that group are regulated; that would be an exemplar or the standard bearer.**

79

So, in other words, a guide is someone who provides us with knowledge we do not have, security we lack on our own, and comfort we cannot give to ourselves. And the most effective guides are the ones who have what we need!

Now, that being said, is it not obvious why there is no guide more wise, more capable, more comforting, more desirable than the Holy Spirit?

After all, the Holy Spirit is more than that; he is Heavenly Father's messenger. Through the Holy Spirit, we are connected both to our Father and our Savior.

Okay, so that makes sense, but how does the Holy Spirit guide us?

The Holy Spirit, as a messenger, conveys to us, through thoughts and feelings, and sometimes through audible words and physical sensation, what Heavenly Father wants us to know and what He wants us to do or not do.

If you do not mind, I would like to share some examples:

One night, a lot of years ago, when we were living in South Carolina, we were traveling home from… somewhere later than we should have been, so naturally, we wanted to get home as quickly as possible. We had planned to take the shortcut route that we usually took, but when we arrived at the intersection where we should have turned, I had a very distinct impression that we should not go that way.

At first it was just a thought, best described by the words, "Do not go that way."

'Why not?' I thought, 'We always go this way.'

But then the thought was accompanied by a strong uneasiness, like a foreboding, the kind of feeling you get when you know something is wrong without knowing what it is that you know.

Well, we did not go that way; we took the long, out-of-our-way route instead, getting home much later than we had wanted to. But the next morning, I learned why the Holy Spirit had been directed to give us that direction.

I saw on the news that, on that road, the one I wanted to take, at the very time we would have been there, there had been a shooting, and several lives ended that night. I knew, as I listened to the news, that, without the Holy Spirit's guidance, that could have, and probably would have been us. He saved our lives.

Another example comes from even longer ago, when we were still living in Pennsylvania. It was time for us to go… somewhere, and I could not find my keys. I looked absolutely everywhere—in the bedrooms, in the kitchen, in the living room, in the bathroom, in the trash, in the dog's bowl, in the toys… you get the idea; but I could not find them. A bit annoyed, I sat down and pouted.

"Where could they possibly be?" I asked myself, and the Holy Spirit answered in words I could actually hear.

He said, "Look in the binding of your photo notebook."

Now, I thought that was silly. Why would they be in my photo notebook? But I did it anyway, and there they were.

I learned, after the fact, that my girls had been playing Hide It, Then Find It (AKA Hide and Seek). Well, they did hide them, but they could not find them, so there they stayed. They had forgotten about them. I, obviously, did not know that they were not where I thought they were, but the Holy Spirit knew, and he told me.

Now, why did he tell me?

Just because I needed them.

Now, if we go back even further in history, to when I was a student at BYU, we find another example.

I had a terrible habit of reading—an actual book—while walking, something like what people do with their cell phones today.

I lived off campus and was walking to class with a book in my hand and in front of my face. I got to East Campus Drive and, without taking my eyes from the page, stepped into the street to cross to the Wilkinson Center. Now, I was so brilliant that I had not even checked for traffic.

Side Note: It is amazing that I have survived myself!

Anyway, as I stepped into the street, I felt what felt like an arm across my stomach, holding me back. Just as I looked up, a car sped past me, nipping the hem of my dress, which was blowing forward. That is how close I was to what could have been a terrible accident.

As I climbed the steps to the Wilkinson Center, thinking about what had happened, I wondered if my Guardian Angel or the Holy Spirit had just saved my life. As I entered the Wilkinson Center, I heard the thought, "Yes, he did! Now be more careful!"

These are just a few examples of how the Holy Spirit directs us and protects us, but he also does more; he teaches and comforts us.

Many times, when I am studying the scriptures, praying, preparing a Family Home Evening packet, or a lesson for Young Women, and I am pondering a particular verse, principle, or concept, its meaning, purpose, and application, suddenly or gradually become very clear. Sometimes, it comes in the form of intellectual understanding, the type you experience in a classroom with a particularly adroit instructor. Other times, I can visualize what I am learning, like watching a PowerPoint presentation.

This does not just happen when I am studying the scriptures; it also happens when I am working on my dissertation or reviewing a patient's case notes, or contemplating what I can do for my children or for someone else, and even when I am seeking to know what more I can do to become more than I am.

This past week, at a girl's camp, he did that for me.

On Monday, I was feeling a bit uncomfortable about going to camp. Unfortunately, I have social anxiety, and even though it is not as bad as it used to be, I still have a difficult time in large crowds and amongst people I do not know. I am also not very good at sitting around doing nothing, but the leaders had no specific responsibilities, so I was apprehensive.

On Tuesday, I felt terrible, so I knelt down in my room in the cabin and prayed. I told Heavenly Father that I knew I should be there, but I did not know why. I asked if there was someone I could help. I asked if I could do something for our Young Women's Leader.

Heavenly Father, through the Holy Spirit, said, "No, but she can do something for you."

I thought, 'Ok,' and then I watched her. I watched her create ways to involve herself, and as I did, I remembered something another sister in our ward had said to me several years ago when I had mentioned that I had been in the ward for over 6 years but still felt like I did not know many of the members. She had said, "Well, Eileen, you need to talk to people."

I knew that she was right, but to tell someone with social anxiety something like that is like telling a flame to keep burning while you are throwing a bucket of water on it. It feels impossible!

But on Tuesday, I felt that Heavenly Father was telling me that I needed to learn to be more than I am by challenging the anxiety and talking to more people than just myself and those I know well, and by stepping out of my bubble and reaching beyond my own arm's length.

Naturally, as always, Heavenly Father did not stop with just the instruction. The rest of the week, He provided opportunities for me to begin to do that, and every time I did, I could feel the Holy Spirit easing my anxiety. He did not just tell me what Heavenly Father wanted me to do; he helped me do it.

In addition to all the guidance, direction, protection, and instruction that we receive through him, he does provide the comfort that we need, when we need it.

Now, if we are receiving what we need, why then is it considered a privilege?

Because Heavenly Father loves us. Because Heavenly Mother loves us. Because Jesus loves us. Neither any of them nor the Holy Spirit will ever abandon us. If we are alone, it is because we have abandoned them.

Because of that love, which is more than we could possibly comprehend, Heavenly Father has given us the privilege, if we will simply accept it, of having the constant companionship of the Holy Spirit.

But we must remember that accepting it also means using it. We must—in all ways on all days—do our best to be our best, not according to the world's standards, nor according to our own, but as given to us through the gospel. We must study the scriptures DAILY!! We must pray, ALWAYS!!! We must live the gospel with exactness, no re-writes, no personal adaptations, no compromises, no amendments, no complaints, no tomorrows, but here and now, and always, in all ways.

In the name of Jesus Christ, Amen!

Live With Gratitude in Your Heart

By

Eileen DiStasio-Clark

November 24, 2024

Olathe 2nd Ward in Olathe, Kansas

Perhaps you have noticed that life is not always easy.

Perhaps you have noticed that life is not always pleasant.

Perhaps you have noticed that life is not always good.

But have you also noticed that, whether things are easy or hard, pleasant or unpleasant, good or not so good, there is always something good to pull from every experience we have, IF that is what we are willing to look for?

I had a nice home in Northland, Missouri. Even though, for the whole of my life, I have always wanted, and still want, a nice little ranch in the country, I never wanted to not have that house because I also wanted it to be the office site of Pursuit of Excellence Institute of Family Education, my non-profit organization.

But, because my Social Security benefit, which is my only source of income, is as small as it is, I was not able to pay the mortgage, so, in order to not lose my house, I had to sell the house. And, of course, that broke my heart and made me cry.

87

But...

Step back in time with me, back to the late 1950s and early 1960s when I was in elementary school. Often, our homework assignments in English and Literature required us to write short stories and poems. Now, though I always loved to learn about everything, and homework was never an annoyance to me, writing stories and poems was definitely my most favorite assignment.

I had not even made it to third grade before I decided I wanted to be a writer and write, and I did! But publish, I could not. As time passed—and a lot of it did—I wondered if that dream would ever come true or if it would just always be a dream.

Now...

Step forward in time with me to December of 2023, when I moved in with my daughter and her husband. That was what made it possible for my dream to come true!

Within approximately four or five months, I was able to accomplish more writing than I had in the previous five or six years. And, in August, I had 27 manuscripts ready for submission to the publisher that Heavenly Father sent to me.

If I had not had to sell my home, that life-long dream and desire to write and publish my works would never have come to pass. You see, I had kept myself very busy doing all I could for everyone I could except myself. Being with my daughter and her husband changed things in a helpful, positive way. For the first time, probably ever, I had time to do the things I so dearly wanted to do, one of them being the publication of 27 manuscripts.

Ergo, in what was one of the saddest trials—having to sell my home—was also hidden one of the greatest blessings—my lifelong dream and desire of having my writings published. So, naturally, in the sowing of heartache, there was the harvesting of great joy!

I believe that is the type of thing **President Dieter F. Uchtdorf** was referring to when he said:

"It might sound contrary to the wisdom of the world to suggest that one who is burdened with sorrow should give thanks to God. But those who set aside the bottle of bitterness and lift instead the goblet of gratitude can find a purifying drink of healing, peace, and understanding."

It really is vitally important for us to know that there is good to be found in all things, regardless of the type of challenges and circumstances that we may be in.

Elder Uchtdorf also pointed out, **"We can choose to be grateful, no matter what.**

"This type of gratitude transcends whatever is happening around us. It surpasses disappointment, discouragement, and despair."

It is always possible to be grateful regardless of what is happening that we would rather not have happened or what is not happening that we would rather have happened.

Heavenly Father blessed me with an amazing immune system, and therefore, I just about never got sick and I rarely ever even felt bad. But, two weeks ago, I became ill. It was the first time in 30 years—literally—that I had become ill, and of course, I did not like it. I prayed and prayed that Heavenly Father would take care of me and that whatever was bothering me would go away quickly. But, instead of a quick recovery, I ended up in the hospital.

Did I like that? No!

Did I appreciate that? No!!

Did I realize there was a purpose to it? No, at least not at first.

But then...

President Jeffrey R. Holland said, **"God hears every prayer we offer and responds to each of them according to the path He has outlined for our perfection."**

What Heavenly Father knew that I did not was that I was where I needed to be with the needs I needed to have in order for Heavenly Father to bless me and others.

Last Sunday, Brother Gotfredson and young Brother Valenti came to the hospital and brought the sacrament to me, after which I was given a blessing. One of the things I was told in that blessing was that through the illness I was experiencing, there was a spiritual purpose for me and others—at the hospital—and my family.

Now, I may not know all that was intended to come from that experience, but I do know this. While talking with one of the Nursing Assistants who tended to me, a gospel conversation arose. Now, this is me. With me, that will always happen. So, that was no surprise. But what was a very pleasant surprise was his interest in what we were discussing and the marvelous spirit I felt at that time.

Ergo, I could see the hand of the Lord in my experience, and I could recognize, with great gratitude, at least one answer to my prayers, which brings me to this point.

We must NEVER forget to REMEMER to pray ALWAYS!!!

Elder Holland has this to say about prayers:

"...our prayers are our sweetest hour, our most sincere desire, our simplest, purest form of worship. ...We are to employ prayer as a shield against temptation, and if there

be any time we feel not to pray, we can be sure that hesitancy does not come from God who yearns to communicate with His children at any and all times.... When we don't know how or exactly for what to pray, we should begin, and continue, until the Holy Spirit guides us into the prayer we should be offering."

Now, with all that said, we must also remember this:

When we pray, we need to choose a private place where we can be alone. We need to free our minds of worry and let go of negative feelings. We must envision Heavenly Father there with us and speak to Him conversationally, from the heart.

We must express our love and gratitude for all that we have received and all that He has already done for us. Then we can express our true and sincere desires and needs! When we do this, as we relax and ponder, we will receive communications with our Heavenly Father that are as clear as a telephone call.

But, let there also be times when we do as **Elder David A. Bednar** suggested:

"Let me recommend that periodically you and I offer a prayer in which we only give thanks and express gratitude. Ask for nothing; simply let our souls rejoice and strive to communicate appreciation with all the energy of our hearts."

In the name of Jesus Christ, Amen!

Every One Is Important

By

Eileen DiStasio-Clark

1987

Characters

Narrator: A Female

Clock: A Male

First Elf: A Male

Second Elf: A Female

Third Elf: A Male

Fourth Elf: A Female

Fifth Elf: A Male

One-Half-of-Eleven: A Male

Other-Half-of-Eleven: A Female

Eight: A Male

Nine: A Male

Twelve: A Female

Thirteen: A Female

Fourteen: A Male

Sixteen: A Male

Scene #1

Carrying their own stools, One-Half-of-Eleven and Other-Half-of-Eleven enter the proscenium from opposite sides of the stage. One-half-of-Eleven enters from Stage Left, and the other half-of-Eleven enters from Stage Right. They sit, dejectedly, on their stools, in Facing Right and Facing Left positions, with their backs to one another.

The Narrator rises from a seat in the left center of the audience and, carrying a sign and easel, ascends the steps to the Right Front Stage. Pausing briefly in front of Other-Half-of-Eleven, she shakes her head sympathetically, then continues left to One-Half-Of-Eleven and places the easel to the left of One-Half-Of-Eleven, where again, she pauses briefly and shakes her head sympathetically, then puts the sign on the easel. The sign reads: "And the Clock Struck Eleven!"

Narrator: Tales have been told, in days of old,

Of clocks striking twelve or one.

In verse or in rhyme, it's always been Time

Ruling "What, When, and How" things are done.

But this is not so everywhere you go,

As in Nature's Control Room,

Where Numbers make the blue of each lake,

And the plants and flowers to bloom.

They make the snow, the winds to blow,

The sun, the clouds . . . all the weather.

Important is their place, so restricted is their space.

For success they must all work together.

But disaster did knock, when good friend Clock

Entered the Restricted Zone. (Pointing to both halves of Eleven)

Now they must get back together to correct the weather,

If nature's to be what we've known.

Scene #2

The curtain opens on a well-lit, happy scene of singing and dancing. A sign, placed center stage, reads, "Nature's Control Room: Authorized Personal Only." One-Half-of-Eleven and Other-Half-of-Eleven, who are smiling and happy, are working on a task.

The Narrator enters the left stage and seats herself on the stool. As the music ends, red lights begin flashing; a buzzer sounds, and a warning is heard from off-stage:

Unauthorized Visitor Approaching

Clock enters Right Stage, dragging his feet and looking very tired.

Narrator: **A bright day was dawning, but Clock was yawning.**

(Clock looks at the Narrator with puzzlement, realizing he forgot to yawn. He then makes an animated effort at yawning.)

All night he'd not been to bed.

His daily agenda gone,

He ended up where he didn't belong,

Because there was confusion in his head.

One-Half-of-Eleven (With minor irritation upon seeing Clock enter the Control Room)

Who let him in? This is a restricted area! (When Clock speaks, no one pays attention to him. One-Half-of-Eleven continues working, but he is obviously bothered.)

Clock:	(Speaking to himself, while searching through his pockets)

Oh, dear me! It just isn't here. I just know I've lost my agenda!

(Runs almost frantically to Upstage Center, where Eight and Twelve are making wind) **Pardon me, but have you, by chance seen a white book? It is my agenda and it is very important!**

[Eight and Twelve search each other's faces questioningly]

Eight:	(With sympathetic concern) **No, Clock, we've been very busy making gusts of wind.**
Twelve:	(With the same concern) **If it would make you happy, I'm sure one of us could stop to help you look...**

First Elf:	(Enters Downstage Right, waving paper as he runs to Eleven) **There's not enough wind in Chicago!** (He exits Downstage Left)
Clock:	(With great alarm, seeing One-Half-of-Eleven's anger, speaking to Eight and Twelve) **No! Don't stop!! I'll find my agenda, if... if I have to search all over town.**
One-Half-of-Eleven:	(Frantic, but still involved at his station) **Someone please get him out of here!**
Clock:	(With desperate gestures and pulling at the hair sticking out of his hat, he heads Downstage Left to Nine and Thirteen, while speaking to himself.) **I'll find it somewhere.** (With a twinge of pain in his expression, he looks at the strands of hair in his hands and rubs his head.) **Ow! And, I hope I find it before I pull out all my hair.** (Clock, looking back at One-Half-of-Eleven, absentmindedly bumps into Thirteen.)

Thirteen:	**Oh! Excuse me! You, I didn't see. Busy I was, making rays.**
Nine:	**We need them, you know; they're not just for show; what else can get through life's dim haze?**
Thirteen and Nine:	(Giggling to each other, obviously pleased with themselves.) **Oh, we're so poetic, aren't we?** (They giggle at their simultaneous dialogue.) **Yes, we are!** (They giggle some more.)
Thirteen:	**Let's try it again.**
Nine:	**OK. You go first.**
Clock:	(Interrupting their fun) **Uh... uh... Please, I've come to ask for your help. I seem to have lost my agenda.**
Thirteen:	**That is bad news! It gives one the blues, not knowing what he should do!**
Nine:	**For what was your list? Will it really be missed? Can you make another anew?**
Thirteen:	(Before Clock has a chance to answer) **He probably could, but less time it would, take to search and find. For**

when making a new one, you never do get done; not everything returns to your mind.

[Thirteen and Nine laugh heartily]

Second Elf: (Enters Downstage Left with another message for One-Half-of-Eleven) **More rays! More rays! They want more rays in the Mojave!**

One-Half-of-Eleven: (To Clock, with irritation) **Are you still here?! This area is for Numbers only! Now get out of here!**

Clock: (Rushing across the stage to Downstage Right, as if to leave, but stops when he gets to Fourteen. He is trying to remain unnoticed by One-Half-of-Eleven, and he looks like he feels a bit ashamed) **I'm a little embarrassed to have to admit it, but I seem to have lost my agenda. You must help me! I'm completely lost without it!**

Fourteen: (As he is working) **I can't help you, but if you consult the big Sixteen, I'm sure he can. He is quite wise.**

Clock: (He heads Upstage Right to Sixteen) **Excuse me, I've been told you are very wise and could probably help me.**

Sixteen: (With pride) **That is correct. If I can't help you, no one can.**

Clock: (With great hope) **Then I certainly hope you can. I always prepare a daily agenda to be sure I get everything done. I have a little white book that I keep all my agendas in, and I know I had it yesterday. But now, I seem to have lost it. I can't find it anywhere, and I don't know what I can do, and…**

Sixteen: (Focusing on a bulge in Clock's hat) **Enough. I can help you. Try looking under your hat.** (Clock, hopefully, and with a little embarrassment showing in his eyes, removes his hat carefully and looks inside. An expression of great relief and joy sweeps across his face as he pulls the book out.)

One-Half-of-Eleven: (In an angry tone) **I thought I told you to get**

out of here! (Clock, quite startled, fumbles with his book and accidentally throws it into the Control Room. He rushes to Center Stage, carelessly searches the floor for his book, repeatedly bumping into One-Half-of-Eleven in a desperate attempt to get his book back. One-Half-of-Eleven is trying to shove Clock out of the Control Room and, at the same time, continue his work.)

Narrator: (Rises from her stool, takes a few steps toward Center Stage, turns to the audience, and while the fumbling is going on behind her...)

Acting without thought, great trouble was wrought,

When Clock angered One-Half-of-Eleven.

(She speaks slowly and deliberately, allowing Clock to follow her direction)

He pushed them and bumped them,

Tripped them and thumped them.

And . . . then the Clock struck Eleven!

(Clock smacks One-Half-Of-Eleven)

That was all One-Half-of-Eleven could take,

This statement he did make...

One-Half-of-Eleven: I positively, permanently quit!

(As the numbers begin to voice alarm)

I won't be abused,

And I am not amused,

By this bumbling idiot!

(He begins to cross to Front Stage Left)

Other-Half-of-Eleven: (Fearfully pleading) **YOU can't leave! This is a job that we've got to perform together. Without your part,**

It may be the start of catastrophes in the weather.

Clock: (Bewildered, he looks at the audience and asks...)

What's with the poetry?

One-Half-of-Eleven: (With determination and indignation, he proceeds to the Narrator's chair)

Don't pull my leg or pretend to beg,

I'm not important around here.

Do my job yourself, or hire an elf.

I really do not care.

[Chimes are heard, signaling to the Numbers that deadlines are close at hand. They scramble back to their positions to continue their work, frantically putting the weather in the wrong places. The lights dim a little. Clock picks up his book and, while reading, exits Stage Left.]

Narrator: (In a hushed voice, as she exits Stage Right, to the audience says...)

Things are different now.

[The rushed activity of the Numbers continues. The Other-Half-of-Eleven is rushing wildly, trying to keep up with the influx of work. A constant stream of frantic elves runs on and off stage, delivering notes to Other-Half-of-Eleven. Appropriate music plays over the action.]

104

First Elf:	**There's too much sun in the Arctic! The oceans are rising! There are floods on all the coast lines!**
Thirteen:	(As he places more rays on the conveyor belt.) **We're hot today! Other-Half-of-Eleven: Well, cool yourselves!**
Second Elf:	**Stop the rains over the Sahara! Are you trying to change the topography of the earth? Why is it snowing in Hawaii?!**
Other-Half-of-Eleven:	(To Second Elf) **I don't know!**
	(To Sixteen, as he dumps more snowflakes and raindrops on the conveyor belt) **Will you please dry up?**
Sixteen:	(Looking a little indignant) **I can't do that. I have quotas to fill and deadlines to meet.**
Third Elf:	**Stop those winds in Japan! It's the wrong time of the year! All the rice fields are being destroyed!**
Eight:	**Look what the wind blew in.**
Other-Half-of-Eleven:	(With irritation) **Well blow out!**

Eight:	**OK! OK! Don't get so huffy.**
Fourth Elf:	**Why are there so many clouds over Oregon?**

Other-Half-of-Eleven: (To Elf; near tears) **I don't know!**

Fifth Elf:	**Those ships are going to crash into the rocks! Stop!!**

Other-Half-of-Eleven: Stop what?!

Fifth Elf:	**Stop what you're doing!**

Other-Half-of-Eleven: I can't!!

Fourteen:	(Dumping more clouds on the conveyor belt) **Tah-Dah!**

Other-Half-of-Eleven: They... OHHH!

Elves:	(All rushing in with messages) **Stop! Stop! Stop! Stop! Stop!**

Other-Half-of-Eleven: (In frantic desperation, he yells...)

STOP!!!!!!

(Cymbals crash)

STOP EVERYTHING!!!!!

(All action freezes. Other-Half-of-Eleven crossed to One-Half-of-Eleven, lights lower behind them. Only One-Half-of-Eleven and Other-Half-of-

Eleven are spotlighted. Other-Half-of-Eleven, placing her arm around One-Half-of-Eleven's shoulder in a gentle, loving voice…)

Things are such a mess. I just can't keep up with everything all by myself. You can't imagine how much I've come to depend upon you. I need you! Please come back!!

Please!!!

[One-Half-of-Eleven ignores the pleadings of Other-Half-of-Eleven.

Other-Half-of-Eleven dejectedly sulks across the stage to where she was

sitting at the start of the play.]

Narrator: (Rising from the audience, she repeats the beginning actions to the Front Center Stage…)

To the start we've returned.

I do hope you've learned;

In order to get the job done—

For just the right weather,

We must all work together,

Yes, it does take everyone.

(Narrator fades back to the darkened stage and writes on a sign, as Other-Half-of-Eleven humming a loving song. One-Half-of-Eleven begins to soften. Realizing they do need each other, he gets up, and begins to cross to Other-Half-of-Eleven. Seeing this, Other- Half-of-Eleven rises, and crosses to One-Half-of- Eleven. They meet Front Center stage, singing together, then return to the Control Room. Narrator crossed to the easel, and places the new sign over the other sign. It reads, "EVERY ONE IS IMPORTANT!" Final production number begins as the normal work routine begins. Curtain closes.

Narrator remains near the easel, smiling until the curtains are completely closed, then exits back to the audience.

THE END

Way Cool Hobbying

By

Eileen DiStasio-Clark

And

S. Michael Clark Junior

1995

A Puppet Show

Written when Michael was 10 years old,

for a Cub Scout Pack Meeting Special Presentation

Characters

Kodiak: a young boy

Pickle: a young boy

Tumbleweed: a young boy

Setting

As the curtains open, Kodiak and Pickle are sitting in Kodiak's back yard. They are trying to think of something to do.

Kodiak: I'm bored.

Pickle: Not as bored as me.

Kodiak: I'm more bored than you.

Pickle: No way!

Kodiak: Yes way!!

Pickle:	No way!!!
Kodiak:	Yes way!!!!

Tumbleweed enters from below, in between Pickle and Kodiak

Tumbleweed:	Which way?
Kodiak & Pickle:	Out of the way!

Pickle and Kodiak push Tumbleweed down.

Pickle:	I'm bored.
Kodiak:	Not as bored as me.
Pickle:	I'm more bored than you.
Kodiak:	No way!
Pickle:	Yes way!!
Kodiak:	No way!!!
Pickle:	Yes way!!!!

Tumbleweed peeks up from below.

Tumbleweed:	I got a way.

Pickle and Kodiak glare at Tumbleweed.

Pickle & Kodiak:	What way?
Tumbleweed:	A way to stop being bored.
Kodiak:	What way is that?
Tumbleweed:	We can find a hobby?
Pickle:	What kind?

Tumbleweed:	Let's look in my dad's cellar. He has lots of things down there.

Kodiak and Pickle follow Tumbleweed down below. From below, they throw things up through the stage, making comments like:

Tumbleweed:	We can collect dolls.
Kodiak:	Dumb way. (Throws it out.)
Tumbleweed:	We can make clothes.
Pickle:	Dumber way. (Throws it out.)
Tumbleweed:	We can sell kisses.
Kodiak & Pickle:	Dumbest way!!! (Throws out Hershey Kisses.)
Tumbleweed:	How about these?
Kodiak & Pickle:	Great way!!!

Together the three come up holding baseball cards.

All Three:	This is way cool hobbying!!!

The End

A Poor Wayfaring Man of Grief

By

Eileen DiStasio-Clark

2003

Adapted as a Play from a Sacrament Presentation

Characters

The Adults Children	The Girls	The Boys	The Young
ANDRINA	Mimi	Gordon	The number of children can vary. They are not speaking parts. They will be singing the song.
DORETTA	Penny	Quincy	
KEITH	Zoey	Ulysses	
WALDO			

SETTING: Narrator is sitting on a stool, in front of the curtain, Stage-Left. On stage, behind

112

the curtain, is a living room setting, with a sofa Back-Center-Stage, a side table with a lamp on each side of the sofa, and two chairs on each side of the sofa: Center Stage Left and Center Stage Right. The middle sofa is facing the audience, and the chairs are facing each other—the chairs on the left are facing right

and the chairs on the right are facing left. On the chairs are seated the adults—2 men and 2 women. On the sofa are seated three of the youth, with the other three youths seated on the floor Center Stage, with several younger children, all of them facing the audience. Those on the floor are seated on pillows. The younger children are holding sheet music. The group is in the process of practicing a presentation for an upcoming event. They all read from a script. At the start of the program, the curtain is closed, and only the front stage lights are on. The curtain slowly opens on the dimly lit stage setting as the Narrator begins to speak.

NARRATOR:　　　Service. Much is said about giving service. Relief Societies all over the church cook dinners when babies are born or someone dies, when someone is ill, and for special occasions. Priesthood groups help move people in and out of almost anywhere, help fix broken cars, and repair or remodel homes. Young Women babysit and go shopping for people who need help. Young Men mow lawns and help to organize garages.

Sometimes these things may be done by assignment; sometimes these things may be done voluntarily. Either way, they are all helpful acts—kind deeds.

But I wonder, what is real service? How do we determine who needs service? How is it determined who gives service? What constitutes real service?

(Stage light go up)

ZOEY:	(Sitting on the floor with the younger children, she leans toward them and quietly instructs them to begin singing) **Now, remember, you will only sing one verse at a time. And when you sing each verse, put your heart into it and sing loud enough to be heard in the back of the auditorium, but soft enough to not be screaming. You sing; I will hum. Got it?**
YOUNG KIDS:	(In unison, they all reply) **Yep! We got it!!** (Zoey then pressed a button on the disc player to begin the music, which she does when each verse is sung. The Young Kids sing and Zoey hums.)

Verse 1

A poor wayfaring man of grief

Hath often crossed me on my way,

Who sued so humbly for relief

That I could never answer nay.

I had not power to ask his name,

Where-to he went, or whence he came;

Yet there was something in his eye

That won my love; I knew not why.

ZOEY: Andrina, begin.

ANDRINA: Under the crumpled newspaper, against the alley wall of Pat's Steaks, he shivered through the chilly Philadelphia night, dressed in the only tattered T-shirt, holey sweater, and ragged corduroy pants he owned.

In the morning, when customers began to arrive, he begged for the price of a cup of hot chocolate. Throughout the day, he made a scanty meal of the scraps left in the sandwich wrappings, often times pulling them from the waste can.

ZOEY: Waldo, you are next.

116

WALDO: Her health had never been good; migraines, depression, ulcers, and diabetes had been with her from her youth. It seemed, with every year, there was another ailment or surgery. Now, leukemia, high blood pressure, and heart disease are taking their toll. Her small social security allowance could not cover the cost of the large price tags on the medication she needed. She was frightened by the number of times she found herself thinking, 'I just can't do this anymore.'

NARRATOR: On our way through this life, we will cross paths

with many different kinds of people. Some will be destitute, some poor. Some will be comfortable, some wealthy. Some of them will have obvious needs and others will have no apparent need at all. We may never know the needs of many of the people we meet. Some in need will not hesitate to ask for help; for others such requests will come with difficulty, perhaps embarrassment. Only after they have done all that they can do, still to find their efforts inadequate, will they humbly go to someone else. We may not understand the need. It may appear that they brought their lot upon themselves. To us, their need may seem as a want. But we must never judge or qualify the petition or the petitioner. All lives are different. Need of those who have had much is quite different from the need of those who have had little. Yet, need is need. The Lord, in John 13:34, commanded us to "love one another". He did not say to love those who love you, or love those who need love, or love those who are loveable. He simply said, "love one another". Without condition, without recompense, we are to love, serve, and help one another.

YOUNG KIDS: (The music begins; kids look at each other. They

sing, Zoey hums)

Verse 2

Once, when my scanty meal was spread,

He entered; not a word he spake,

Just perishing for want of bread.

I gave him all: he blessed it, brake,

And ate, but gave me part again.

Mine was an angel's portion then,

For while I fed with eager haste,

The crust was manna to my taste.

ZOEY: Doretta, it is your turn.

DORETTA: He had come up from poor circumstances, working hard for every penny he earned. Now, he was one of the wealthier men in Arlington. While serving as Ward Mission Leader, he was introduced to a young woman who was rich in spirit but poor in possessions. She was embracing the gospel readily, yet she would not come to church. Sensitive inquiry revealed her reason to be the lack of proper clothing for herself and her children. He took his wife to Jacksonville's finest clothing store, and then, after they completed their shopping spree through the Missionaries, they presented a wardrobe of Sunday outfits to this gentle mother and her children.

ZOEY: Now you, Ulysses.

ULYSSES: For years it had been her practice to save all her coins and $1.00 bills. It was her way of making sure that there was some kind of fun for the kids. They were not poor, but they never really had much more than the necessities, and her husband was often out of work. This being one of those times that money, the money that she had accumulated by saving their coins and $1.00 bills, was their only opportunity for a little summer enjoyment. But, when car troubles stranded a Utah-bound family of seven, close to her home, she offered to help in anyway she could, not really knowing what there was she could do. A call came from the mother; they had noting to eat.

"Is there anything you could do to help us?" she asked. The woman thought for a moment, then remembered the money she had been saving since Christmas. She took them to the grocery store and let them buy what they could. Before she left for home, she gave them several $20.00

bills for gas money. After a few more requests for help, she found that the savings that had been meant for her family had been totally depleted. But still, as she drove away from the hotel for the last time, she counted herself the greater blessed. No feeling, no possession, and no amount of savings could compare with the love she felt from Father in Heaven.

NARRATOR: Some people in need will not ask for help; pride is their ally. Some people in need expect help; ungratefully, they feel others owe it to them. But the humble needy, petitioning for help only after they have done all they can do, or accepting help for which they did not have to petition, bless the giver with sincere gratitude and love. Then, follow the Lord's blessings: an increased sense of worth to others, to self, and to our Heavenly Parents, and peacefulness and fulfillment in our own times of need. With everything to give, or nothing at all, there will come opportunities to serve, to give of ourselves, our substance, and our love. May we give, not hesitatingly, but with sincere compassion.

ZOEY: Okay, Mimi.

MIMI: It was a cold February night on which she waited, a mother, with her son, outside the grocery store for her daughter to get off work. Bad news from the night-before had been reaffirmed that day, and weighed heavily on her mind, as she and her son sat in the van, both wondering the same thing, 'What will we do now? How will we take care of ourselves?'

Their attention to their own situation was diverted by the figures of a poor woman, dressed in dirty, warped, and worn clothing, barely suitable for the temperatures, and a small child, dressed in like manner. They watched silently as the sad pair walked, searchingly, over the parking lot, finally approaching the van. She opened her window to the cold night air and the woman's

desperate plea for money. "Please help us," the woman begged. Without hesitation or thought of her own circumstances, she took out her wallet and gave all the money she had to the woman, apologizing for the little that it was. Then, as she watched the pair continue their quest, she thought of the change she kept in the van. She circled the parking lot and pulled up beside the woman and child. Through her open window, she offered all the rest of the money she had to the poor woman, who accepted it gratefully. As she returned to the curb, her son quietly asked, "Mom, have you ever wondered if people like that really need help or if they just do that to get money?"

"I suppose there was a time when I did wonder," she frankly replied, then thoughtfully added, "it really does not matter, though. I do not need to know; the Lord knows. He will judge them for their honestly, and us for our charity. I do not need to know if their need is real; I just need to give, or at least be willing to give, if I cannot."

NARRATOR: If ever you might think to judge the need first, perhaps you would give thought to Mosiah 4: 17-25: 17. Perhaps thou shalt <u>say</u>: The man has brought upon himself his misery; therefore, I will stay my hand, and will not give unto him of my food, nor impart unto him of my substance that he may not suffer, for his punishments are just—18. But I say unto you, O man, whosoever doeth this the same hath great cause to repent;

and except he repenteth of that which he hath done he perisheth forever, and hath no interest in the kingdom of God. 19. For behold, are we not all <u>beggars</u>? Do we not all depend upon the same Being, even God, for all the substance which we have, for both food and raiment, and for gold, and for silver, and for all the riches which we have of every kind? 20. And behold, even at this time, ye have been calling on his name, and begging for a <u>remission</u> of your sins. And has he suffered that ye have begged in vain? Nay; he has poured out his <u>Spirit</u> upon you, and has caused that your hearts should be filled with <u>joy</u>, and has caused that your mouths should be stopped that ye could not find utterance, so exceedingly great was your joy. 21. And now, if God, who has created you, on whom you are dependent for your lives and for all that ye have and are, doth grant unto you whatsoever ye ask that is right, in faith, believing that ye shall receive, O then, how ye ought to <u>impart</u> of the substance that ye have one to another. 22. And if ye <u>judge</u> the man who putteth up his petition to you for your substance that he perish not, and condemn him, how much more just will be your condemnation for withholding your substance, which doth not belong to you but to God, to whom also your life belongeth; and yet ye put up no petition, nor repent of the thing which thou hast done. 23. I say unto you, wo be unto that man, for his substance shall perish with him; and now, I say these things unto those who are rich as pertaining to the things of this world. 24. And again, I say unto the poor, ye who have not and yet have sufficient, that ye remain from day to day; I mean all you who deny the beggar, because ye have not; I would that ye say in your hearts that: I give not because I have not, but if I had I would give. 25. And now, if ye say this in your hearts ye remain guiltless, otherwise ye are condemned; and your condemnation is just for ye covet that which ye have not received.

YOUNG KIDS: (As the music begins, they hum and then sing, Zoey hums)

Verse 3

I spied him where a fountain burst

Clear from the rock; his strength was gone.

The heedless water mocked his thirst;

He heard it, saw it hurrying on.

I ran and raised the sufferer up;

Thrice from the stream he drained my cup,

Dipped and returned it running o'er'

I drank and never thirsted more.

ZOEY: Quincy.

QUINCY: Though they were working hard to save money for adoption, the gift of her husband's tuition reimbursement checks had provided the opportunity for her mother, brothers, and sisters to go Christmas shopping, and for another sister to come home for the holidays. "But you need that money," her mother had said. "You needed the money you gave to us when we needed help," she had replied. The overtime money had bought food, gas, and little things for them throughout the months of no income. When there was no money for her mom to pay the mortgage, they emptied their savings account.

With their reserves gone, they still sought ways to help.

NARRATOR: "Sometimes the very thing you're looking for is

the one thing you can't see." Words from a song, yet truth. Indeed, sometimes we are so close to the solutions and blessings we seek, yet we do not recognize them. The reasons for such a handicap are as varied as the people troubled by it. Often it takes the love and perspective of another to help us see, show us the way, or walk the path with us. We may not always know what or how much another person needs. But if we take direction from the Lord, and walk with them to the end of the path, until the Lord says let go, they will have been blessed and helped, and we, most likely, will find our good deeds will return to us, and we will be possessors of divine and eternal rewards.

YOUNG KIDS: (They begin to hum with Zoey and then sing; Zoey hums)

Verse 4

'Twas night; the floods were out; it blew

A winter hurricane aloof.

I heard his voice abroad and flew

To bid him welcome to my roof.

I warmed and clothed and cheered my guest

And laid him on my couch to rest,

Then made the earth my bed and seemed

In Eden's Garden while I dreamed.

ZOEY: Now you, Penny.

PENNY: Luke 10: 30-3530…. A certain *man* went down
from Jerusalem to Jericho, and fell among
thieves, which stripped him of his raiment,
and <u>wounded</u> *him,* and   departed,
leaving *him* half dead. 31. And by chance, there
came down a certain priest that way: and when
he saw him, he passed by on the other side.
32. And likewise, a Levite, when he was at the
place, came and looked *on him,* and passed by
on the other side. 33. But a certain <u>Samaritan</u>, as
he journeyed, came where he was: and when he
saw him, he had <u>compassion</u> *on him,* 34. And
went to *him,* and bound up his wounds, pouring

in oil and wine, and set him on his own beast, and brought him to an inn, and took <u>care</u> of him. 35. And on the morrow when he departed, he took out two pence, and gave *them* to the <u>host</u>, and said unto him, Take care of him; and whatsoever thou spendest more, when I come again, I will repay thee.

NARRATOR: The storms of life take many forms: health issues

or financial problems, emotional trials or physical challenges, abuse, neglect, loneliness… and more. You can too ease the burdens of others and raise their spirits and outlook, but only if you are standing on higher ground yourself. Since every life is peppered with personal trials, if we are to lift others out of the seas of affliction we must be standing upon the Dock of the Gospel. Love so that the Spirit can whisper guidance to you, guidance for you and for others. Hold true to and live worthy to use the Lord's principles. Sometimes, requests for help will come to you; be ready! More often, you will need to offer that help: be willing.

YOUNG KIDS: (The youth sitting with them sing with them)

Verse 5

Stript, wounded, beaten nigh to death,

I found him by the highway side.

I roused his pulse, brought back his breath,

Revived his spirit, and supplied

Wine, oil, refreshment—he was healed.

I had myself a wound concealed

But from that hour forgot the smart,

And peace bound up my broken heart.

ZOEY: Gordon, it is your turn.

GORDON: If a house needed fixing, he was there with a hammer and saw. If a lawn needed trimming, his mower was on the move. No tears fell among his friends or associates without landing on his shoulders. His money put young men on missions, sent couples to the Temple, and repeatedly aided the needy. He seemed to have the solutions to problems before people knew they had the problems. His own life's storms could not stop him from helping others. Not until he was laid to rest, and probably not even then, did his service to others end.

NARRATOR: As recorded in Matthew 16:24, the Savior

taught, "If any man will come after me, let him deny himself, and take up his cross, and follow me." President James E. Faust taught this: "Taking up one's cross and following the Savior means overcoming selfishness; it is a commitment to serve others. Selfishness is one of the baser human traits, which must be subdued and overcome. We torture our souls when we focus on getting rather than giving." Elder William R. Bradford once said, "Of all influences that cause men to choose wrong, selfishness is undoubtedly the strongest. Where there is selfishness, the Spirit of the Lord is absent. Talents go unshared, the needs of the poor unfulfilled, the weak un-strengthened, the ignorant untaught, and the lost unrecovered." There are many times in a person's life when service seems impossible to give; we have our own needs to tend, those we seek to help seem to refuse us, and help rendered to other ends in injury to us. Yet, always, we must focus on giving.

YOUNG KIDS: (They sing with the music, Zoey hums)

Verse 6

In prison I saw him next, condemned

To meet a traitor's doom at morn.

The tide of lying tongues I stemmed,

And honored him, 'mid shame and scorn.

My friendship's utmost zeal to try,

He asked if I for him would die.

The flesh was weak my blood ran chill,

But my free spirit cried, "I will!"

ZOEY: Keith, now you.

KEITH: "On June 18, 1844, Joseph Smith mobilized his troops to protect Nauvoo.... Illinois governor, Thomas Ford, apparently sided with the opposition... and ordered the Church leaders to stand trial... this time in Carthage. Joseph and Hyrum first considered appealing to U.S. President John Tyler, but then decided instead to cross the Mississippi and escape to the West. Pressured by family and friends who felt abandoned and who believed Joseph to be nearly invincible, he agreed to return and surrender; but he prophesied that he would be going "like a lamb to the slaughter" and would be murdered in cold blood." Joseph urged Hyrum to save himself and succeed him as a prophet, but Hyrum refused and accompanied his brother to Carthage. Despite his promises of protection and fair trial, Governor Ford allowed the Smiths [and Williard Richards and John Taylor] to be imprisoned by their enemies without bail and without a hearing on a wholly new charge of treason for having declared martial law in Nauvoo. Stating that he had to "satisfy the people," the Governor ignored clear warnings of danger and disbanded most of the troops. He then left the hostile Carthage Greys to guard the jail and took the most dependable troops with him to Nauvoo." On June 28th, [they] "All… felt unusually dull and languid, with a remarkable depression of spirits. In consonance with those feelings, [John Taylor} sang a song, that had lately been introduced into Nauvoo, entitled, "A Poor Wayfaring Man of Grief"… The afternoon was sultry and hot. The four brethren sat listlessly about the room with their coats off, and the windows of the prison were open to receive such air as might be stirring.

Late in the afternoon, Mr. Stigall, the jailor, came in and suggested that they would be safer in the cells. Joseph told him that they would go in after supper... Hyrm Smith asked Elder Taylor to sing again, "A Poor Wayfaring Man of Grief."[Elder Taylor replied,] "Brother Hyrum, I do not feel like singing."[Hyrum said,] "Oh, never mind: commence singing and you will get the spirit of it."Soon after finishing the song the second time, as he was sitting at one of the front windows, Elder Taylor saw a number of men, with painted faces, rushing round the corner of the jail towards the stairs "...a mob of between one hundred and two hundred armed men—many of them from the disbanded Warsaw Militia—blackened their faces with mud and gunpowder, and then stormed the jail. In less than two minutes, they over came feigned resistance from the Greys, rushed upstairs, and fired through the closed door. Hyrum, [who was] shot first, died instantly, [John Taylor, an Apostle], tried to escape out a window and was shot five times, but survived to later become the Church's third President. Only Willard

Richards, another Apostle, survived unharmed. Trying to go out the window to deflect attention from the two survivors inside, Joseph Smith was hit in the chest and collarbone with two shots from the open doorway and two more for outside the window His final words, as he fell to the ground outside the jail, were, "O Lord, my God!"

NARRATOR: What we esteem as being of great value is the good and desirable that we do not possess. Upon that principle, understanding life's purpose, we can conclude that that which is of greater value than life itself, which we do possess, is the Gift of Exaltation, which we do not now possess. What we do have is the promise to have all that is good and of real value; love, family, knowledge, and joy eternally, to live the kind of life God lives, with the kind of authority, power, knowledge, wisdom, and perfection God has, to create, to be like God. To realize this promise, we must give everything to the Lord: obedience to his commandments—all of them—repentance for our sins—all of them—honesty and truthfulness in our dealings and words—all of them—service to his children—all of them.

ALL CAST MEMBERS: (All cast members stand and sing)

Verse 7

Then in a moment to my view

The stranger started from disguise.

The tokens in his hands I knew;

The Savior stood before mine eyes.

He spake, and my poor name he named,

"Of Me, though hast not been ashamed.

These Deeds shall thy memorial be;

Fear not, thou didst them unit Me."

NARRATOR: N. Eldon Tanner counseled: "Let us look for the

good rather than try to discover any hidden evil." That is the key to seeing the Savior in those we serve. If we look to find fault in others, we will find it. We then, will never see the Savior. If, instead, we look for something good, we will find it. We then, will come to know the Savior even better. Since every person has qualities unique to themselves, and all good is of the Lord, each time we look for the good, we find another quality of our Lord. As we implement those qualities in our own lives, we are bettered. Look for those to serve; don't wait for an assignment or request. Give all you can give, expecting nothing in return, yet be grateful for the blessings you receive. Do all you can do for yourself. But in your times of need, when your efforts alone, are not enough, accept the love and help of others. Be grateful! Then, when you can, return the kindness to another. Great rewards await those who serve the Lord, for those who do not, great sorrows. Matthew 25: 31-46 teaches:31. When the Son of man shall come in his glory, and all the holy angels with him, then shall he sit upon the throne of his glory: 32. And before him shall be gathered all nations: and he shall separate them one from another, as a shepherd divideth his sheep from the goats: 33. And he shall set the sheep on his right hand, but the goats on the left.34. Then shall the King say unto them on his right hand, Come, ye blessed of   my Father, inherit the kingdom prepared for you from the foundation of the world:35. For I was an hungred, and ye gave me meat: I was thirsty, and ye gave me drink: I was a stranger, and ye took me in:36. Naked, and ye clothed me: I was sick, and ye visited me: I was in prison, and ye came unto me. 37. Then shall the righteous answer him, saying, Lord, when saw we thee an hungred, and fed thee? Or thirsty, and have thee drink? 38. When saw we thee a stranger, and took *thee* in? or naked, and clothed thee? 39. Or when saw we thee sick, or in prison, and came unto thee? 40. And the King shall answer and say unto them, Verily I say unto you, Inasmuch as ye have done *it* unto one of the least of these my brethren, ye have done *it* unto me. 41. Then shall he say also unto them on the left hand, Depart from me, ye cursed, into everlasting fire, prepared for the devil and his angels: 42. For I was an hungred, and ye gave me no meat: I was thirsty, and ye gave me no drink: 43. I was a stranger, and ye took me not in: naked, and ye clothed me not: sick, and in prison, and ye visited me not. 44. Then shall they also answer him, saying, Lord, when saw we thee an hungred, or athirst, or a stranger, or naked, or sick, or in prison, and did not minister unto thee? 45. Then shall he answer them, saying, Verily I say unto you, Inasmuch as ye did *it* not to one of the least of these, ye did it not to me. 46. And these shall go away into everlasting punishment: but the righteous into life eternal.

FINALE: The Narrator steps back on the stage with the rest of

the cast. As the song, "A Poor Wayfaring Man of Grief" —music only—plays, and the curtains are closed slowly. When the song ends. the lights go out. Then, after a short moment, the auditorium lights go on.

The End

Once Upon a Might Have Begun

By

Eileen DiStasio-Clark

Late 2004

SCENE   Relief Society Meeting: four women are seated on stage Right-Center, facing Left; the Chorister stands Left-Center, facing women seated; the Relief Society President sits behind to the left of the other women.

AT RISE: Chorister, standing before the Sisters, conducts them in the singing of "As Sisters in Zion." At the conclusion of the hymn, the Relief Society President assumes the position of the and the Chorister sits in the President's seat

R. S. PRESIDENT: I'd like to excuse Sister Lee, who is visiting out of town this week, and thank Sister Novac for filling in as our chorister. As you know, March is the birthday month of the Relief Society. It has been 162 years since the sisters of Nauvoo organized themselves to provide service to each other and to members of their community. So, the next time you find yourselves up to your elbows in laundry, with five kids to get to there different activities, which all begin at the same time, dinner to fix before your husband gets home, and the Compassionate Service leader calling with an assignment for you to take dinner to a family across town, just take a few moments to thank the sisters of Nauvoo. (Everyone chuckles softly)

No, in truth, I am grateful to be a member of the Relief Society. It has brought a lot of meaning and purpose to my life, and has made it possible for me to have wonderful relationships with many fine women from whom I have learned much over my years as a member of the church.

I will now turn the time over to Sister Novac, who has prepared a special and somewhat creative lesson for us today about the birth of the Relief Society. (Sister Novac picks up her portfolio and exits the Right corner of the proscenium, stands behind a music stand, as if giving a lesson; stage lights go down, footlights go up, as curtains close, the cast exits Stage Right)

NARRATOR: Once upon a long time ago, in the beautiful city of Nauvoo, Illinois, There lived a tiny little woman. (Rosa enters auditorium on the Right, strolls leisurely toward the stage) Actually, we have no idea how big or little she was. We do not even know who she was; we just know that she was. We may suppose that she was new to the town and wanted to get to know the other women of Nauvoo. Why? ...Why not?! It was the thing to do in those days—get to know your neighbors ~ friendliness was a habit back then. As a matter of fact, it seemed there were other women in Nauvoo who felt the same way. (Deborah and Naomi enter the auditorium on the Left, strolling leisurely toward the stage, meeting Rosa at the steps, Center Stage)

ROSA: Good morning, sisters. Well, I guess you are not really my sisters; I do not have any real sisters, just brothers, nine brothers. I do notknow why I had nine brothers. Brothers do make life… well, interesting. But brothers! Oh, brother! What can I say about brothers? Uh, side note here; I am just kidding. My brothers are great! Of course, sisters would have been a nice experience too, but then, I guess you are kind of my sisters. So, sisters, how are you today?

DEBORAH: Quite good, thank you. Quite good.

NAOMI: Very well, indeed, and you; how are you? Then again, who are you?

ROSA: Oh, I am Rosa and I am fine too. Well, how I am is not Rosa, and who I am is not fine. I am fine when you ask how, and Rosa when you ask who. I guess you could say I am a fine Rosa (she chuckles a little at herself and the others chuckle with her). And who are you and you?

DEBORAH: I am Deborah and this is my neighbor, Naomi.

NAOMI:	Are you new here?
ROSA:	Oh no; I have been around since I was born.
	(Everyone chuckles again) But I have just come to Nauvoo. Well, not just. I got here about a week ago. You are the first sisters I have met, except for Phoebe, my sister-in-law, but then I knew her before. I would like to get to know more of the sisters. Do you have a sewing circle or parlor group?
DEBORAH:	Well, we were just discussing how nice it would be to organize a society for the sisters of Nauvoo. We could strengthen the sisterhood of all the women here and perhaps do some good for one another.
NAOMI:	There is always a need for benevolent works. Wouldn't you agree?
ROSA:	Why, yes! As a matter of fact, Phoebe could be your first benevolent work. She is ill and must stay in bed for a time. She said to me, just last night, how nice it would be to be able to visit with the

sisters. She misses their company and conversation.

DEBORAH: Perhaps we could visit with her now?

NAOMI: Yes, let's do that! (Stage light go up as the curtains open; the sisters exit up the stage steps)

SCENE: A cot is upstage left; there is a chair by the cot and a small table just behind the right arm of the chair; a basket of laundry is in between the chair and the cot; a broom leans against the back of the table; a dust cloth is on the table.

AT RISE: Phoebe is lying on the cot. The sisters cross the stage to her. Rosa sits in the chair. The other sisters begin to sweep and dust. Rosa olds laundry as they talk.

PHOEBE: Oh, how good it is to see you! Sit. A visit with friends is just what I need. (As the narrator speaks the three women take turns conversing silently with Phoebe, dusting, sweeping, and folding laundry)

NARRATOR: The power of love was not a mystery to the people of earlier times. The art of conversation, the magic of friendship, the uplifting effects of compassionate service were trademark traits of those caught up in the human experience. Among the women of Nauvoo, there was not a longing for corporate success, athletic recognition, public praise, or self-gratification; rather, they sought to give comfort, build and strengthen relationships, and improve lives. Even the smallest of needs were not overlooked.

PHOEBE: Sisters, could I ask a small favor of you? One of the things I miss most while I am away from meetings is the music. Would you sing to me? (Rosa, Deborah, and Naomi converse silently between themselves, then sing the first verse of "Abide With Me"; curtain closes, sisters exit Stage Left; chair and table, with the lamp are moved into position on the proscenium, Stage Right; Eliza R. Snow enters Stage Right and sits, reading, in the chair, the four sisters enter Stage

	Left, crossing the proscenium to Eliza R. Snow; they converse silently)
NARRATOR:	It wasn't long before a group of women, seeking to form a society for the promotion of sisterhood and the organization of benevolent service, asked Eliza R. Snow to draft a constitution and bylaws for such a society. Sister Snow was agreeable to the idea and willing to accept the assignment. (Eliza rises; they all exit together; Stage Left: chair, table, and lamp are removed) When Joseph Smith learned of this, he asked that the sisters be called together so that he could provide "something better for them than a written Constitution."
SCENE:	Stage light go up as the curtains open; six women are seated stage Center Stage Right, facing Left; Joseph Smith stands Center Stage Left, facing the women
AT RISE:	Joseph Smith is addressing the sisters.

JOSEPH SMITH: "I will organize the women under the Priesthood after the pattern of the priesthood. I am deeply interested that [the Relief Society] might be built up to the Most High in an acceptable manner. When instructed, we must obey that voice… that the blessings of heaven may rest down upon us—all must act in concert or nothing can be done—that the Society should move according to the ancient Priesthood." (Footlights go down, Narrator resumes character of Sister Novac, crosses to Center Stage Left; Joseph Smith exits Stage Left)

SISTER NOVAC: And so it was; on March 17, 1842, the Relief Society was organized as an auxiliary of the Melchizedek Priesthood. The sisters quickly began their service. They obtained work opportunities for the needy, took in the homeless, and made donations to help those in need of food, shelter, and schooling. The work of society blessed everyone. There was not a need ignored nor a heart overlooked.

Sisterhood flourished, and learning increased. Joseph Smith promised, "If you live up to your privileges, the angels cannot be restrained from being your associates." Today, women and their families bask in the blessing attendant to the associations of angels as they continue to serve, learn, and fellowship in the Relief Society organization—one of the great gifts of a loving Heavenly Father to us is His daughters on earth.

The End

www.ingramcontent.com/pod-product-compliance
Lightning Source LLC
Chambersburg PA
CBHW060233030426
42335CB00014B/1437